BLOOD ON THE PRAIRIES
Cadaver of a Crow Indian, slain and scalped near the Boundary Line, 1873.

Across the vast undulating prairie

INDIAN CAMP ON OLD MAN RIVER (WEST OF FORT MACLEOD, ON A FLAT KNOWN AS SAMPLE BOTTOM)

came the photographer

PHOTOGRAPHERS' CAMP ON INTERNATIONAL BOUNDARY SURVEY, 1874

Adventurers, veterans of the U.S. Civil War, and officially-appointed cameramen recorded the North American West for posterity—and for a variety of employers. The railroads and boundary commissions frequently hired pioneer photographers to travel West with their "mirrors-with-a-memory," chemicals (here being ground by the photographer whose candid camera caught the scene), assorted tripods, glass plates, printing paper, a wagon for a darkroom, and even fresh water for developing. (For the very professional photographer, however, travelling was not so inconvenient: F. Jay Haynes, officially covering the building of the Northern Pacific Railroad, acquired his own Pullman photographic car.)

to factually record the tragedies

FUGITIVES FROM THE GREAT MINNESOTA UPRISING OF 1862. PHOTOGRAPH (FROM A STEREOSCOPIC CAMERA) BY J. E. WHITNEY

To capture "views of Indian life" was photographer Whitney's rationale for venturing west. He arrived in Minnesota one day before the massacre erupted, however, and what he has depicted here is the despair and anxiety of the white refugees fleeing from the Sioux.

Indirectly, though, Whitney did in fact make his pictorial statement on 'Indian life.' Exploited by government and individual alike, the hate brewing within the Indian was such that the Sioux Chief, Little Crow (while fully aware that his people stood no chance whatsoever against the government), knew that "trouble with the whites must come sooner or later. It might as well be now."

The white man had failed to fulfil his promises, and the war of revenge was to last three months and claim the lives of 644 settlers; many refugees were to seek asylum in Canada.

CROW INDIANS KILLED BY BLOODS IN THE SWEETGRASS HILLS, 1874

The name of the range was sadly deceiving, for in the early '70's, the Sweetgrass Hills was a haven for fugitives—and frequently, a zone of terror. Here a scout observes the aftermath of tribal rivalry.

the despair...

SASKATCHEWAN'S INAUGURAL CELEBRATIONS, 1905
The Mounted Police, who had nurtured the new western provinces, escort Governor General Earl Grey to Regina.

and the triumphs

where this legend was born.

A golden treasury of those

Mountie
1873-1973

early years

Dean Charters

Introductory Sections by Angela M. O'Connell

Collier-Macmillan Canada, Ltd.

Copyright © 1973 by
Collier-Macmillan Canada, Ltd.

All rights reserved.
No part of this book may be
reproduced or transmitted in any form
or by any means, electronic or
mechanical, including photocopying,
recording or by any information
storage and retrieval system without
permission in writing from the
Publisher.

02.973420.7 (hardcover)
02.973400.2 (paperback)

Design: Golden Salmon Estb. Co.
Library of Congress Catalog Number
72-92332

Collier-Macmillan Canada, Ltd.
1125B Leslie Street, Don Mills,
Ontario

Macmillan Publishing Co., Inc.
New York

Printed and Bound in Canada
5 4 3 2 1   77 76 75 74 73

NON COM'S FORT WALSH, 1880

BULL TRAIN FROM FORT BENTON TO FORT MACLEOD, 1879

The trail between the two forts represented the principal trade route of the region. Until the arrival of the Canadian Pacific Railway, Mountie and merchant alike were dependant upon the bull and this route. Benton was the steamboat terminus on the upper Missouri River (about 100 miles below the Canadian border).

Contents

Pictures are grouped in the patterns of a photo album. The introductory text, appearing between groupings, will provide general continuity.

Preface	24
Introduction	25
Chapter 1	31
Chapter 2	109
The Riel Rebellion	157
Chapter 3	199
Chapter 4	239
Postscript	249
Chronology	251
Credits	253

N.W.M.P. PATROL GUARDING THE FRONTIER DURING THE RIEL REBELLION, 1885

Commissioner Irvine, in his report of the campaign, spoke highly of the men under his command. Pictured fourth from the left is Supt. McIlree, who "efficiently commanded the division serving at Maple Creek and Medicine Hat. The duty of scouting the Cypress Hills and adjoining country to the south and west was very thoroughly done, with good results."

Acknowledgements

The Mountie romance was recorded by the men who travelled west with their "mirrors with a memory." To the photographer and to the Mountie (often one and the same) this book is dedicated.

Grateful acknowledgement is extended to the Glenbow-Alberta Foundation, the Public Archives of Canada, The Ernest Brown Collection – loving memory banks, all.

COLIN FRASER, PROUDLY PERUSING HIS PELTS ($30,000 WORTH!)

Preface

The year 1973 marks the centennial anniversary of the Royal Canadian Mounted Police. With such a glorious history to remember, it is certain that many celebrations will take place and many tributes will be paid. This book is one of them. A number of comprehensive histories have been written about the Mounties. This is not just one more. It does not strive to tell the complete story of the force, but is, rather, a pictorial tour of adventure through those glorious early days.

One hundred years is not long when we are talking about history, but a glance at these photographs shows the phenomenal growth of this country of ours during that period. Small wooden forts surrounded by a stockade to protect the inhabitants from marauding Indians, are now the sites of huge cities. The vast herds of buffalo that roamed the prairies have long since vanished. Hundreds of miles of desolate prairie have been transformed into modern farms utilizing the latest machinery, and are helping to feed a hungry world. Even the forbidding wasteland of the Arctic is giving up its treasure of natural resources.

And the man who laid the groundwork for this phenomenal growth was the Mountie. Without his work of pacification, the task of settling and civilizing the west could not have been carried out.

The photographers who took these pictures must have been imbued with the same spirit of adventure that motivated the Mountie. The proof is here. Wherever the men of the N.W.M.P. went, the photographers followed. The results of their work are here on these pages and are, we think, a fitting tribute to the men of the Royal Canadian Mounted Police.

Introduction

It was a year like many others, the year of 1873. Great men were born, others died. Important and trivial events were recorded in the history books. It was the Victorian era, and in England that august lady who gave her name to the period prepared for a visit from the Shah of Persia. Disraeli waited impatiently in the wings to serve his beloved monarch and Napoleon III died at Chislehurst at the age of 64. The Sultan of Zanzibar abolished slave markets and there was famine in Bengal. The Remington typewriter was produced and the process of colour photography discovered. Leo Tolstoy started to write *Anna Karenina* and Sergei Rachmaninoff was born. While exploration of the continent of Africa continued, Livingston died in England and Stanley was received by the Queen. In the United States of America the Union Pacific and Central Pacific railways had linked up at Promontory, Utah in 1869, and the vast American west was opening up to a strangely uncivilized brand of civilization.

And in the Dominion of Canada, Parliament was grappling with the problems of putting a young nation together and making it work. A Boundary Commission had started its work the year before. The resources of the Treasury were small and the demands upon it heavy. There had been those troublesome Fenian raids from the south, the organization of two new provinces, Manitoba and British Columbia, and there was a promise to be fulfilled to the latter—a railway to be built that would tie together that sprawling mass of heterogeneous districts, peoples and cultures.

There was enough to occupy the mind of Canada's first Prime Minister, Sir John A. Macdonald, but he must have taken the time to worry about other problems facing the new country, because when he rose in the House on May 23, and proposed the formation of a police force to maintain order in the rowdy west, he knew exactly the type of force he wanted.

It was to be a para-military mounted police, modelled on the Royal Irish Constabulary. His choice of the RIC as model was probably based on the opinion that if this type of organization could cope with the Irish, it was bound to have some effect on the wild Indian.

When an order-in-council was passed on August 30, and the North West Mounted Police was born, he appointed an Irishman to be its first Commissioner. Lieutenant-Colonel George Arthur French was an officer of remarkable energy and vigour, we are told. He sported an enormous waxed moustache, which perhaps may account for the popularity of such adornment as shown in the photographs of the original members of the force.

Superintendent James Farquharson Macleod, a graduate in law from the Queen's College, Kingston, was appointed Assistant Commissioner.

Sir John was also specific about the design of the uniform for the Mounties – he wanted as little gold lace and fuss and feathers as possible.

The pay scale ranged from a salary of not more than $2,600, and not less than $2,000 for a Commissioner down to $1.00 a day for a constable and 75 cents per day for a sub-constable.

The motto of the new force was "Maintien le Droit", and the duties involved in maintaining the right were clear. To stop the liquor traffic among the Indians, to gain their respect and confidence, to break them of their old practices by tact and patience, to collect customs dues, and to perform all the duties of a police force.

The man who agreed to do all this for the handsome wage of 75 cents per day must have been, in view of what he accomplished, a special kind of man. Some of course had seen regular service in the civil police, the Canadian Artillery, the Canadian Militia and the Royal Irish Constabulary, but there were also among them we are told, clerks, tradesmen, soldiers, farmers, telegraphers, sailors, gardeners, lumberjacks, professors, bakers, butchers, surveyors, university students and one bartender.

One who joined up a few years later went on to write a book about his experiences. He was Corporal John G. Donkin and in his book he describes the type of man who chose this life.

"After having been about two months in the corps, I was able to form some idea of the class of comrades among whom my lot was cast. I discovered that there were truly 'all sorts and conditions of men'. Many I found, in various troops, were related to English families in good position. There were three men at Regina who held commissions in the British service. There was also an ex-officer of militia, and one of volunteers. There was an ex-midshipman, son of the Governor of one of our small Colonial dependencies. A son of a major-general, an ex-cadet of the Canadian Royal Military College at Kingston, a medical student from Dublin, two ex-troopers of the Scots Greys, a son of a captain in the line, an Oxford B.A., and several of the ubiquitous natives of Scotland, comprised the mixture. In addition, there were many Canadians belonging to families of influence, as well as several from the backwoods, who had never seen the light till their fathers had hewed a way through the bush to a concession road. They were none the worse fellows on that account, though. Several of our men sported medals won in South Africa, Egypt, and Afghanistan. There was one, brother of a Yorkshire baronet, formerly an officer of a certain regiment of foot, who as a contortionist and lion-comique was the best amateur I ever knew. There was only an ex-circus clown from Dublin who could beat him. These two would give gratuitous performances nightly, using the barrack-room furniture as acrobatic 'properties'."

Another interesting man who turns up during accounts of the Riel rebellion is the man in charge of Fort Pitt, an Inspector Francis Dickens, son of Charles Dickens. He had at that time under his command 20 Mounties. We are told that when Big Bear surrounded the fort with 250 armed Indians demanding arms and supplies, Inspector Dickens could do little else than refuse and evacuate the fort under cover of darkness. He and his men escaped in a leaky boat, and after six days of gales on the freezing Saskatchewan River, they reached Fort Battleford. Dickens, evidently lacking his father's literary ability, wrote in his diary, "Very cold weather. Travelled."

Perhaps it was this versatility in the make-up of the Mounties that accounts for the amazing success they had.

One of their initial tasks when they set out from Dufferin on the morning of July 8, 1874 was to locate and deal with the notorious Fort Whoop-Up. This establishment was located six miles from the present site of Lethbridge, Alta. It was a fort in every sense, protected by a stockade and guarded by a muzzle-loading brass cannon and a six-pound howitzer, and flying over it all, the Stars and Stripes. It was owned and operated by one Johnny Jerome Healy, a six-foot-two Dublin man who concocted a mixture of whiskey, chewing tobacco, red pepper, Jamaica ginger and molasses and traded it to the Indians for anything they had to offer. One cup of this 'fire-water' bought a buffalo robe; a quart would purchase a pony or even a daughter.

The orgies that took place regularly just outside the gates of Fort Whoop-Up make ancient Roman parties look like Methodist meetings. Johnny Healy was said to employ a small army of rum-runners, the strength of which was said to be anywhere from two to five hundred men. It was thirteen of these men, who in the summer of 1873, drunk on their own wares, massacred thirty Assiniboine men, women and children at a place called Cypress Hills. This massacre and the indignation it produced had influenced Sir John A.'s decision to form the new force.

The march westward was enough to discourage anyone. During the two month period, the men of the North West Mounted Police encountered black flies so numerous that they clogged their nostrils, a prairie thunderstorm described as one continuous flash of lightning that lasted from 10 p.m. to 6 a.m. and led to a stampede of their horses, and fleas that infected every man from the Colonel down. Their food ran low, and eventually each man was rationed to 14 ounces of flour and a dried slice of potato per day. Their water came from buffalo sloughs, and after being boiled and filtered, was still the colour of ink. Behind them was a trail of dead horses, abandoned equipment and frozen oxen. The men began to call themselves the "dismounted police". Their guide was so unreliable that Colonel French remarked, "I am not certain whether his actions are due to ignorance or design. He is the greatest liar I have ever met, and is suspected as a spy of the Whoop-Up villains.... I begin to feel very much alarmed for the safety of the force."

When they finally located Fort Whoop-Up, after having obtained a new guide from Fort Benton, they found that Johnny Healy had flown, taking refuge south of the border. The only occupant of the Fort was one of his henchmen, who with typical western hospitality, invited the troops to dinner. It was the kind of victory that the Mounties were to win over and over again as they spread westward, establishing forts and carrying out their police duties. Their very presence seemed to inspire respect from the Indians and fear among the lawbreakers.

But it couldn't have been as easy as it sounds. Until the North West Mounted rode in, the white man encountered by the Indian had for the most part been interested only in his exploitation. The Indian approached these newcomers in the red coats, first with curiosity and then with trust, and the cultivation of this trust must have required a diplomacy and delicacy not often found in men trained to fight.

It was to pay off when in 1876 the Blackfoot were invited by their neighbours to the south, the Sioux, to join them in a war against the U.S. Cavalry. The Blackfoot curtly declined. And later, after the 7th United States Cavalry under General Custer was wiped out and Sitting Bull and Crazy Horse, along with 5,600 Indian men, women and children sought refuge in the Dominion, a situation that could have been explosive was handled and solved.

The attitude of the Indian to the Mounties was probably best expressed after the signing of the Great Blackfoot Treaty in 1877. After the treaty was signed, Chief Crowfoot rose and made the following statement: "The advice given me and my people has proved to be very good. If the police had not come to this country where would we all be now? Bad men and whisky were killing us so fast that very few of us would have been left today. The Police have protected us as the feathers of the bird protect it from the frosts of winter."

With the coming of settlers to the prairies, the duties of the N.W.M.P. changed, or perhaps a better word would be broadened. They fought prairie fires, became customs officers, rescued victims of winter blizzards, helped the ill and the victims of accidents, arranged weddings and funerals, carried the mail, captured murderers and kept a weather eye on lumber, mining and railroad construction camps. They probably delivered babies also, if called upon. And one of their major duties at this time was to move their old friends, the Indians, to reserves far away from the Boundary. The building of the railway brought large gangs of construction men to the west. They were a rough, brawling group and again the diplomacy and tact of the mounted policeman was needed to settle disputes among the railway workers and between them and the Indians.

The Indians and half-breeds saw their buffalo herds disappear before their eyes with the coming of civilization. The Métis, with the settlement of Manitoba, moved westward to Saskatchewan, only to find civilization hard on their heels. With the buffalo gone, they turned their hand to farming and then watched helplessly while surveyors parcelled out their land. Their pleas to Ottawa went unheeded. Their natural leader, Louis Riel, returned from exile in the States, where he had gone after the Red River uprising, and trouble was inevitable. The first clash of the North West Rebellion came between Riel's forces and the Mounties based at Prince Albert. Superintendent Crozier, in charge of the fort led his forces into an ambush at Duck Lake. Twelve of his men died and eleven were wounded and he was forced to retreat.

For the first time, the Indians saw the redcoats defeated and the results were instantaneous. They attacked white settlements; a few inhabitants who were unable to reach the safety of Mountie forts were slaughtered, and the North West Rebellion was in full swing.

An army was raised in the east and put under the command of a 60-year old retired British soldier, Major General Frederick Dobson Middleton. This gentleman, lacking any knowledge of the terrain or the Métis, refused advice from anyone except ex-Imperial officers "of good birth". Had he taken better advantage of the 500 mounted cavalry of the N.W.M.P., the best in the country, perhaps the rebellion would have been even shorter than it was. They were used mainly on patrols and as advance guards, drawing the fire of the enemy, a position that must have seemed familiar to the 'riders of the plains'.

After the collapse of the North West Rebellion, and the completion of the C.P.R., the emphasis on the prairie was on settlement and the establishment of the trappings of civilization. Again, the versatility of these men of the Mounties was put to use.

They expanded their activities to the North and when the Yukon gold rush occurred, their duties ranged from carrying the mails to scattered mining camps to the pursuit of murderers.

And when the Yukon became a little tamer, the Mounted Police pushed ever farther north, opening posts even in the sub-Arctic. Perhaps that's why it seems so strange today to see a Mountie directing traffic at an airport. A Mountie is out of place in an urban setting. The history of this country shows him always one step ahead of civilization. In 1903, while carrying dispatches in the Arctic a young constable was caught in a vicious winter storm. When his body was found, it was discovered that he carried a scrawled note in the pocket of his scarlet tunic. It seems to typify the spirit of the whole force. It read, "Lost, horse dead. Am trying to push ahead. Have done my best."

TRANSPORT TRAIN FOR THE INTERNATIONAL BOUNDARY COMMISSION, 1874
Royal Engineers, a corps of Mounted scouts (chiefly made up of halfbreeds), and some 300 "young Canadians and old Countrymen" filled the various positions in the commission. Commissioner of the boundary survey was Captain D. R. Cameron, R. A.

CANADA'S FOUNDING FATHER, SIR JOHN A. MACDONALD

Chapter 1

The time between the years 1873 and 1880 must have been the most difficult for the fledgling police force. Many of the men were inexperienced and even to those who had served with other forces the trials of those early years were formidable. There were the vast areas of inhospitable territory to be covered, the extremes of weather peculiar to the Canadian west, the flies, the fleas, the hunger, the white lawbreaker to be hunted and prosecuted and the effects of his demoralizing effect on the Indian countered. And perhaps most disturbing of all was the uncertainty of their reception by the Indians.

The Mountie must have known that if he were unsuccessful in winning over the Indian, the rest of his work would be almost impossible. The degree to which he succeeded in this, his most difficult task, would be shown in later years. The redcoat was the harbinger of civilization and civilization would bring the devastation of the traditional way of Indian life. The buffalo herds, the main source of Indian food and clothing disappeared, the 'free' range became the cultivated prairie, and eventually the Indians themselves would be confined to reservations.

Despite this, the Blackfoot Confederacy was to remain steadfast in its loyalty to the force during some of its most trying times.

As the railway inched its way across the prairie, close behind came the settler—the farmer, the small businessman, the tradesman, the adventurer. The Mountie was the law to all of them; not only the law, but help in time of trouble and friend in time of joy.

SEATED: CAPT. JOHN FRENCH. INSP. FRANCIS DICKENS (SON OF CHARLES DICKENS) IS SPORTING A BEARD, 1874

On the Prairies, a letter from a loved one back home was a special—but not a very frequent—treat. And so, according to Mountie apocrypha, many of the men formed "letter-sharing clubs". Here Capt. James "Corky" Criswell (?) waits his turn to read a letter from his girlfriend Molly.

LIEUT.-COL. GEORGE ARTHUR FRENCH,
FIRST COMMISSIONER

COL. W. D. JARVIS, INSPECTOR OF N.W.M.P.

FORT GARRY AND THE "S.S. DAKOTA" 1871

Ft. Garry actually was the Old Hudson's Bay Company's post built in 1821 (an annex was constructed in 1835) at the junction of the Red and Assiniboine Rivers. Here, Winnipeg was 'conceived,' and here she spent her formative years.

CANADIAN MILITIA ARTILLERY GROUP, 1872
Fort Garry Barracks, Winnipeg. Captain Cotton sitting on a gun trail (centre).

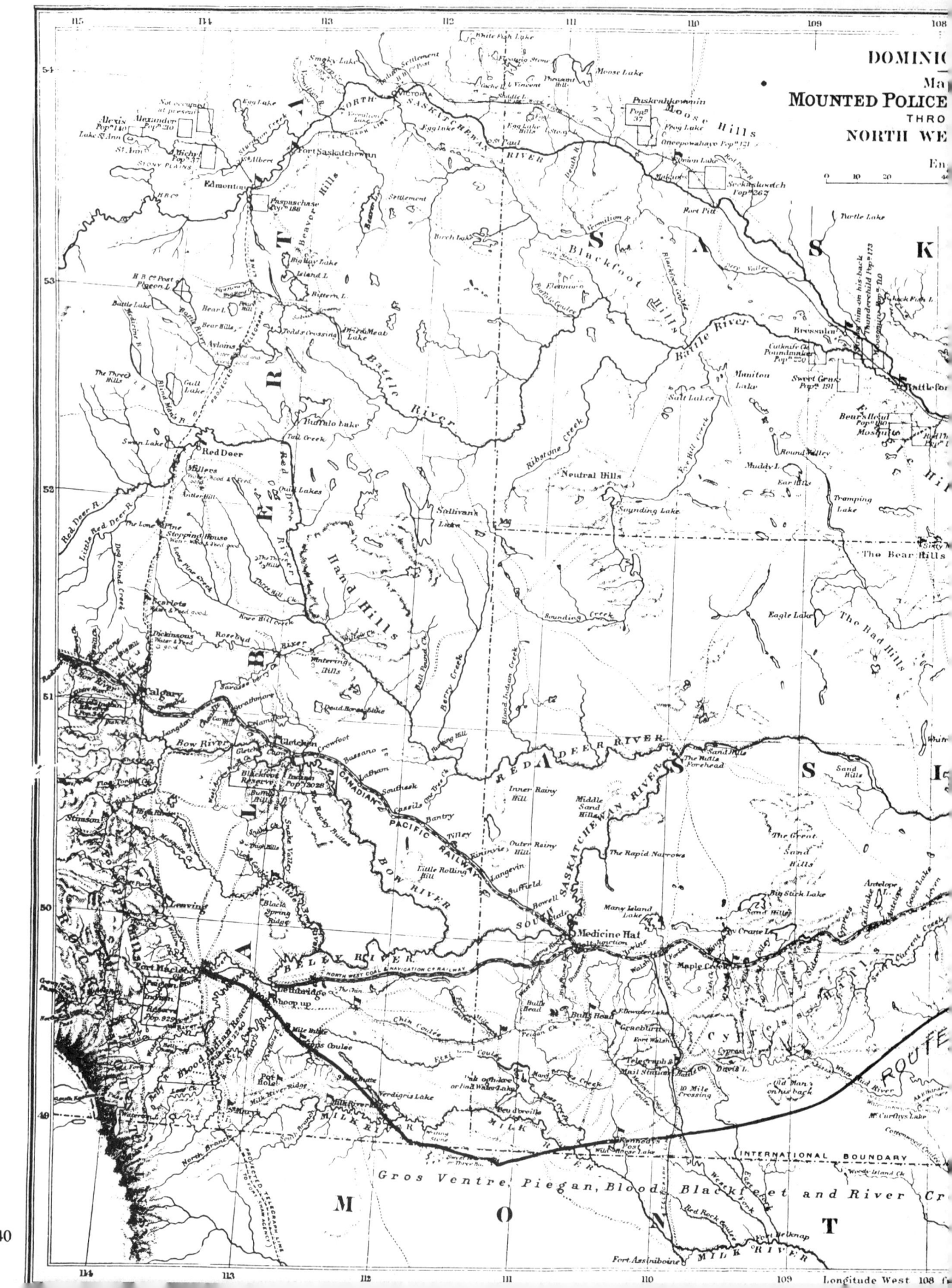

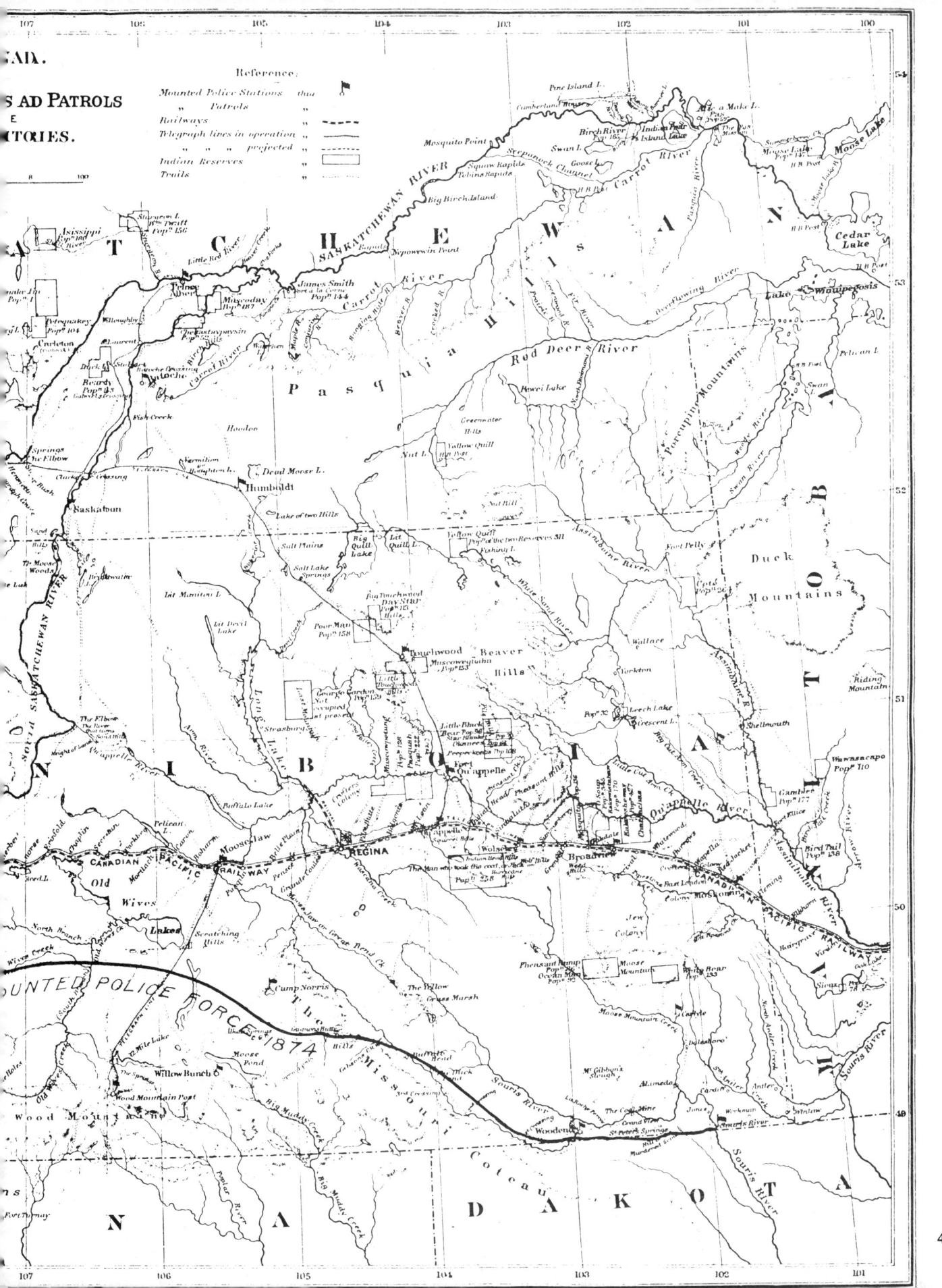

BLOOD INDIANS AT FORT WHOOP-UP, 1870's (NOTE U.S. FLAG FLYING. THE FLAG ALSO WAS NOTED—WITH SURPRISE—BY ASST. COMMISSIONER MACLEOD AND HIS TROOP UPON THEIR ARRIVAL, OCTOBER 9, 1874)

Fort Whoop-Up, in southern Alberta, was the scene of illegal trading and a centre of debauchery and violence. Here, drink-crazed Indians 'exchanged' their buffalo robes and furs for the white man's 'fire-water'.

Originally called Fort Hamilton, the name soon gave way to the more colourful "Whoop-Up". One story goes that when an assistant had gone to Fort Benton for supplies, he was asked—"How's trade?"—and replied—"We're whooping it up." When he set out to return, someone remarked—"He's going back to whoop-it-up.".

Fort Hamilton was erected by two Fort Benton traders—Hamilton and Healy—and it was located on the junction of the Belly and St. Mary's Rivers. Soon after its construction, it was destroyed by fire. Rebuilt with a strong blockade, the new fort boasted ramparts, loop-holes, and massive gates.

The notorious Whoop-Up was the central point of reference in the strong recommendation (1872) presented by Col. P. Robertson-Ross (Commanding Officer of the Canadian Militia), whereby Ottawa was advised that a customs house on the Belly be erected and that there be established " . . . one regiment of mounted riflemen . . . as sufficient to support the government in establishing law and order. . . ."

When they arrived in 1874, Asst. Commissioner Macleod and his men were greeted by the sole occupants: a decrepit Civil War veteran and one or two Indian squaws.

D. W. DAVIS, M.P. ALBERTA (FIRST M.P. TO BE ELECTED FROM THE NORTH-WEST TERRITORIES)

Davis was elected in Alberta's first federal election, February 22, 1887. A Conservative, he sat in Canada's Sixth Parliament. Manager for I. G. Baker and Company (Macleod), he was one of the earliest traders to reach the Blackfoot country. Although not present, Davis was in charge of 'Whoop-Up' when the Police first arrived.

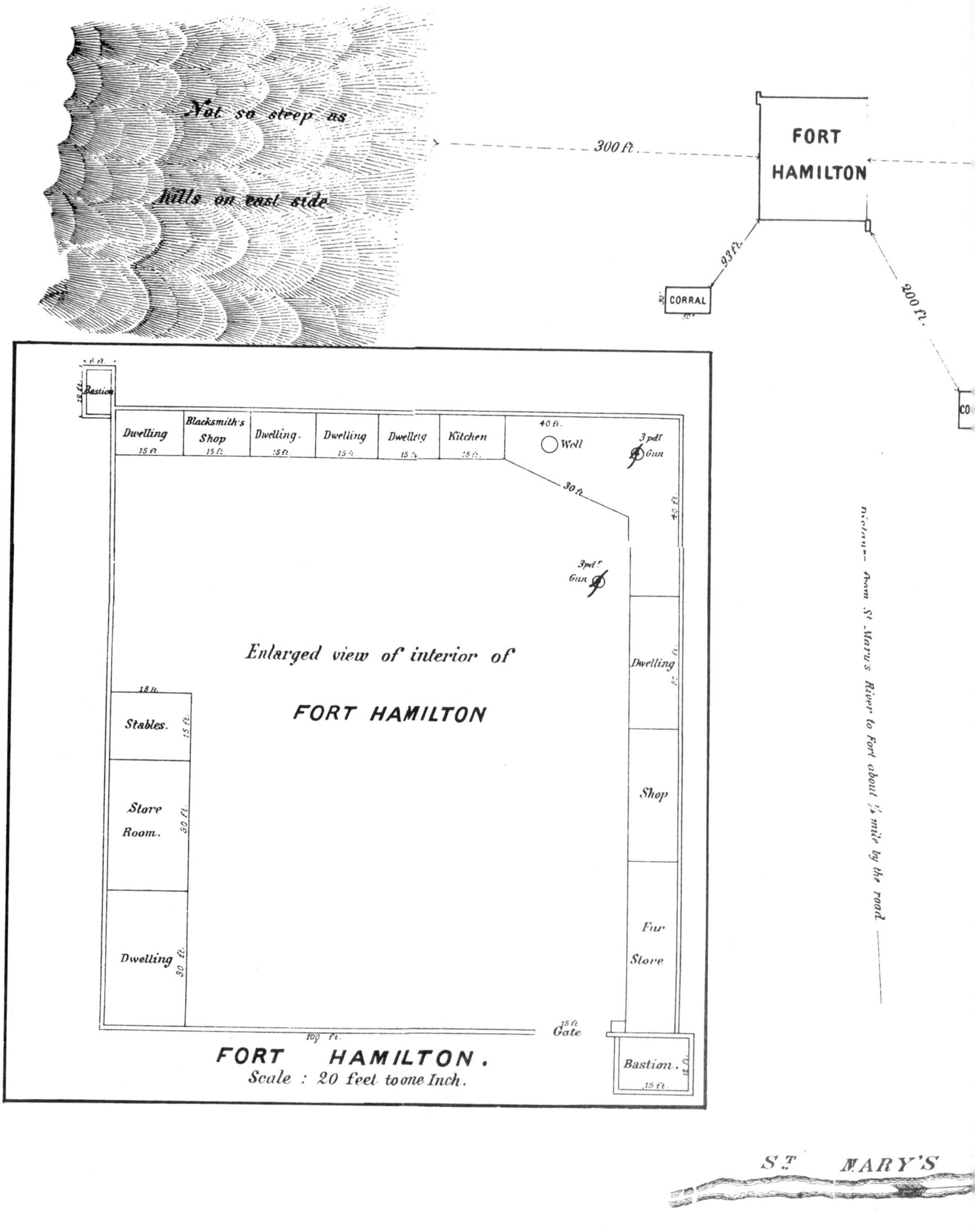

Not so steep as hills on east side

300 ft.

FORT HAMILTON

93 ft.

CORRAL

200 ft.

Bastion 16 ft. 18 ft.

| Dwelling 15 ft. | Blacksmith's Shop 15 ft. | Dwelling. 15 ft. | Dwelling 15 ft. | Dwelling 15 ft. | Kitchen 15 ft. | 40 ft. ○ Well | 3 pdr Gun |

30 ft.

40 ft.

3 pdr Gun

Dwelling

Stables. 18 ft. 15 ft.

Store Room. 50 ft.

Enlarged view of interior of

FORT HAMILTON

Shop

Dwelling 30 ft.

Fur Store

100 ft.

Gate 15 ft.

FORT HAMILTON.
Scale: 20 feet to one Inch.

Bastion. 18 ft. 15 ft.

Distant from St. Mary's River to Fort about ½ mile by the road

ST. MARY'S

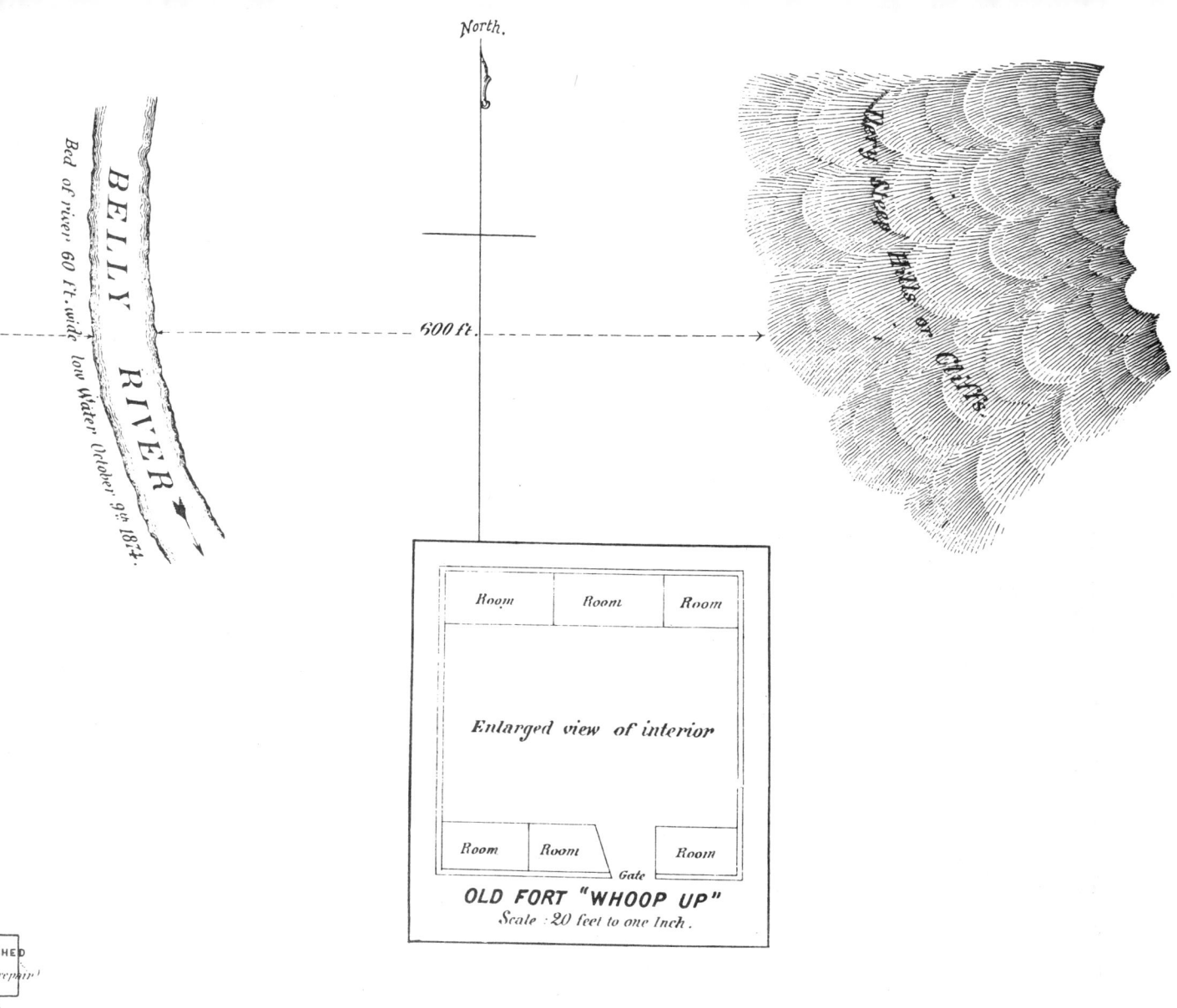

MAIN STREET—HELENA MONTANA, 1870

Formerly known as Last Chance Gulch, the name of the roaring Montana mining town was changed when the residents decided that it was no longer a dignified appellation. Tradition has it that it was decided to rechristen the town "Helena" in honour of Mrs. Gumpertz (Helena) Goldberg, then the only 'respectable' white woman around. A more official theory for the origin of the name is that it comes from Helena, Minnesota, the hometown of one of the miners.

This 'miner's capital' was connected by overland trail to Ft. Benton, on the Missouri. The incredibly irresponsible courtroom procedures of Helena, the shooting affrays, the dance halls (and worse), all contributed to the notoriety of the town.

THE INIMITABLE JERRY POTTS. FORT MACLEOD

Integrity, loyalty and artfulness were the qualities that earned this famous scout, interpreter and guide deep and lasting admiration. Respected by Police and Indian alike, Potts himself was the son of a Scot fur trader and a Piegan Blackfoot squaw.

On at least one occasion Potts served as war chief to his Indian brothers:—in the autumn of 1870, when the Cree attacked the Blackfoot. The Blackfoot were afflicted with smallpox and were outnumbered, but panic stricken Cree were eventually scattered across the Belly River valley. Jerry, who returned from the affray with nineteen scalps, a deep head wound of his own (for 22 years a 2B shot pellet lodged in the lobe of his left ear), an arrow lodged in his body— and imperishable fame, capsulized the victory: "You could fire with your eyes shut and be sure to kill a Cree."

Potts' assurances to the Indians that the arrival of the Police indicated overdue equal justice for Indian and white smoothly paved the arrival of the Mounties. During the erection of Fort Macleod, Potts was influential in stopping illegal trading, particularly of liquor.

A colourful scout, a venerable drinker, a superb rider and a wise mediator, Jerry Potts depicted the Renaissance man of the Canadian West.

A loving husband, deeply devoted to his family, Commissioner Macleod, the 'private' man, conveyed his feelings in a letter to his wife, Mary, dated October 1877.

My Dearest Mary:

I have just got back to this place (Fort Walsh) with Sitting Bull and a lot of his chiefs. It was quite a job getting them this far, they are so suspicious. However here they are safe at the fort, about 25 of them. I expect General Terry at the boundary (Fort Benton) on Sunday and am going out to meet him myself. I hope to get through with them on Tuesday or Wednesday and then if possible I will start for home. How I do look forward to getting there, day and night. Winder writes by Mr. Power that you were not well. I sincerely hope it was only that cold you spoke about. Perhaps you will see me before you see this. The messenger is waiting for my dispatches, so good-bye my own darling

I am, as ever,
Your own Jim

Mary J. Macleod, often alone while her husband was on duty, possessed the inner strength and outward resourcefulness of the Pioneer Woman. In 1877, she was a witness to the signing of the Great Blackfoot Treaty (No. 7). In 1881, she graciously received His Excellency the Marquis of Lorne, Governor General of Canada. For that occasion, Mary Macleod wore an ensemble from her 'finery wardrobe' of one: a black plush coat trimmed with silver fox. Unfortunately though, the material had worn at the elbows. Undaunted, she blackened her arms with charcoal and warmly welcomed His Excellency.

N.W.M.P.—MEDICINE HAT, 1875

BULL'S HEAD, CHIEF OF THE SARCEES AND A PRINCIPAL SIGNER OF TREATY NO. 7 (GREAT BLACKFOOT TREATY), 1877

CROWFOOT, HEAD CHIEF OF THE BLACKFOOT CONFEDERACY

Crowfoot, chief of the entire Blackfoot confederacy, eloquently spoke of the Mounties as having protected the natives "as the feathers of a bird protect it from the frosts of winter... I will sign the treaty." Red Crow, head of the Bloods, reaffirmed these sentiments. Bull's Head replied, "We are all going to take your advice."

RED RIVER SETTLEMENT HOMES, 1870's

N.W.M.P. SERGEANTS; CIRCA 1870'S; LIKELY AT FORT MACLEOD

BUFFALO BONES NEAR LLOYDMINISTER (Chief Poundmaker's last Great Corral, circa 1874)

CHIEF POUNDMAKER

Poundmaker earned his name through his 'management' of Buffalo pounds. In these corrals, the animals were captured and slaughtered.

SUPERINTENDENT JOHN COTTON

Superintendent of the Prince Albert district, Cotton's "F" Division was noted for being crime-free. Cotton himself gained personal recognition for advocating that the helmet ("wretched headdress") be dropped from the official Mountie uniform. He also favoured a uniform of neutral colour. In his report for 1892, he stated that ".... A Mounted Policeman can now enforce the laws of the Dominion, and this without loss of prestige in any uniform, be it a buckskin suit or a homespun garment...."

Cotton served as Lieutenant in the Fort Garry Garrison in 1873. In 1881, he held the distinction of escorting His Excellency to the Father of all Mounted Police Posts in the Far West, Governor General Lorne, to Fort Macleod.

Supt. Cotton is pictured, minus chapeau, circa 1875.

N.W.M.P. PARADE, FORT MACLEOD, 1875

Looking at the photo, you are at the north end of the street, facing southwesterly. The slough is about two hundred yards south of town. The Old Man's River is on the west of town. Turning to the right, on the north of town, it is some hundred yards to the N.W.M.P. barracks, going easterly towards Lethbridge. The old town was completely surrounded by water, and subjected to high floods when the snow melted in the mountains during the spring. While the floods were in progress, no one could leave the Island or any persons, even the mail, could be delivered to town. On one occasion the ferry-boat was carried away, taking the cable and supports along with it for some distance. The Powers-that-be at the time decided to move away to where the present town is now situated, relieving the anxiety caused by the floods. (Above description by W. J. Ryan of Macleod, Alberta.)

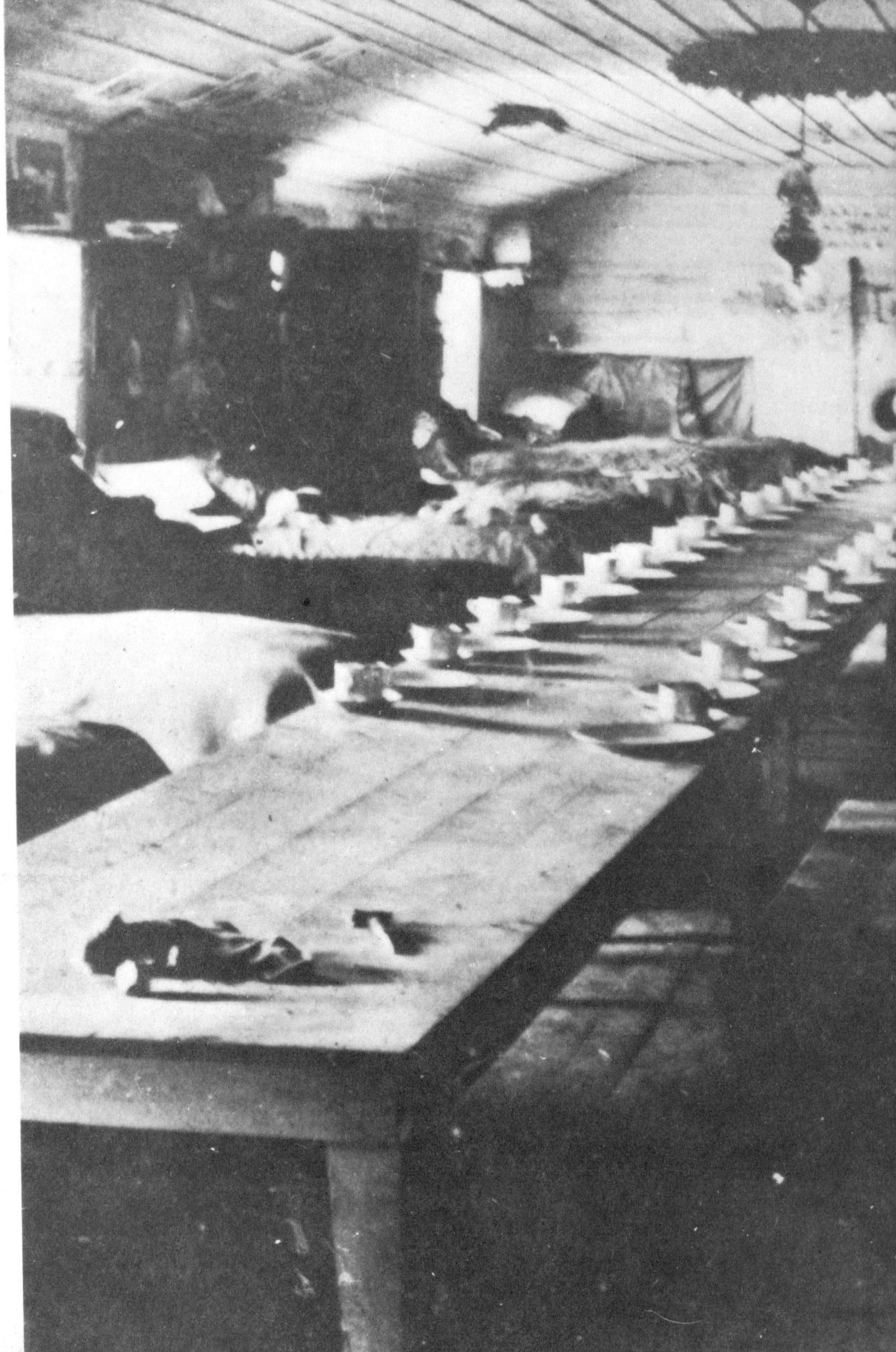

C TROOP MESS AT FORT MACLEOD, INTERIOR VIEW, 1879

IN
MEMORY
of
FRANK BAXTER
F. Div N.W.M.P.
Died
17 JAN 1875

THE GRAVES OF WILSON AND BAXTER
On New Year's, 1875, these men lost their lives while riding from Fort Macleod to Fort Kipp.

INDIAN ENCAMPMENT NEAR CALGARY

FORT WALSH, CYPRESS HILLS, 1878

Because of the persisting whiskey trade—now moved from Whoop-Up to the Cypress Hills—it was decided that Supt. Walsh leave Fort Macleod to establish and command a Fort of his own, named after himself. Jerry Potts directed the course of the journey. His instructions were to head for the 'massacre ground on the headwaters of Battle Creek,' and the destination was reached June 7, 1875. A display of a warlike front by several of the younger Sioux Indians greeted the troop. Warnings from the older members that the police camp would be cleaned out prompted Walsh to reply—"Should you attempt to do so, very soon there will be more redcoats than there are buffalo." The Indians dispersed, a threatening situation was averted, but Walsh's words were to prove sadly ironic. Soon indeed – within a single decade – the buffalo, image of an indestructible throng, were virtually to disappear.

S. J. CLARKE, N.W.M.P., 1876

Pictured at Fort Walsh, S. J. Clarke wears plainsman's costume, an outfit that suited the hard life the Mounties led on the plains.

FIRST N.W.M.P. BAND AT FORT WALSH, 1879

The first musical aggregation of the Mounties was set up by a voluntary group in 1876 at Swan River, Manitoba. The instruments for it were hauled in by dog team from Winnipeg. Depicted here is the band that was formed at the suggestion of the First Commissioner, George A. French.

N.W.M.P. OFFICERS AT FORT WALSH, 1876
Back row: S/Insp. Neale, S/Insp. Dickens, S/Insp. Antrobus, S/Insp. McIllree, S/Insp. Frechette, S/Insp. Denny. Middle row: Lt. Col. Irvine, Lt. Col. Macleod, Dr. Kittson. Seated in front: S/Insp. Clark.

TWO BLACKFOOT WARRIORS AT FORT WALSH, 1878

CAPT. FRED YOUNG (LEFT) AND CAPT. G. S. MOFFATT AT FORT WALSH

SAM GRAVEL

A time when a man rode across the barren plain at full gallop. A time when right and wrong were easily distinguished. Pictured is Sam Gravel, whose name alone, suggests a proud cowboy in a real-life adventure story.

AN UNIDENTIFIED SCOUT

ALLEGED TO BE THE LAST PARADE OF CUSTER'S CAVALRY BEFORE THE "MASSACRE"

Sitting Bull (Ta-tan-ka Yo-tan-ki), son of a Hunkpapa (Sioux) chief, was reputed to have killed his first opponent while yet a child. That fight resulted in an injury which made him permanently lame; hence, the derivation of his name. A foremost medicine man and diplomat, he was to become the political leader of the Sioux tribes.

"The Great Spirit made me an Indian, but he did not make me an agency Indian, and I will not be one." So spoke the Chief who was to lead his immense following in the immortalized Custer Massacre (a misnomer) in 1876. While technically a Sioux victory, this was the battle that ended the Sioux as an independent entity. The tribes scattered, fleeing in every direction; Sitting Bull himself fled to the only available haven: Canada.

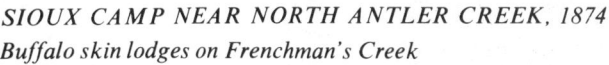

SIOUX CAMP NEAR NORTH ANTLER CREEK, 1874
Buffalo skin lodges on Frenchman's Creek

GALL: SIOUX WAR CHIEF, 1879

Gall, the Hunkpapa (Sioux) war chief had played a major role in defeating Colonel George Custer at Little Big Horn. A meditative man, the Chief was among the followers of Chief Sitting Bull and Medicine Bear who had fled to Canada following CUSTER'S LAST STAND. The celebrated Chief Gall was eventually to preside over most of the Sioux.

FAR LEFT, SIOUX CHIEF RAIN IN THE FACE

South of the border, Indian distrust of agents was continually rising, assuming dangerous proportions. The stories of native unrest travelled into Canada. One of these rumours was that Chief Rain In The Face had virtually taken over the Fort Peck Indian Agency. Consequently, the Mounties exerted even greater efforts to maintain a strict watch. In Rain In The Face's situation, it was refusal by a local agent to feed any more Indians that prompted rebellion. In Canada, the dearth of buffalo meat was also yielding hunger—and potential unrest.

SPOTTED EAGLE, LEADER OF THE SANS ARCS. SECOND IN IMPORTANCE TO SITTING BULL AMONG THE SIOUX
The knife he is holding is now in the R.C.M.P. museum at Regina.

RIGHT: SLEEPING BULL, A CHIEF OF THE SIOUX
The Chief is clad in warrior's dress, and is holding a captured U.S. cavalry sword.

A MOUNT AND HIS MOUNTIES

Although the scene is pure MGM, the fellow dressed up for the Wild West movie is actually Constable Fred Young. To complete the picture is Cp. G. B. Moffatt lying on the ground. And, of course, the third member is a Blood Indian. The set: Fort Walsh.

FORT WALSH, 1877
Drill with 7 pound guns (Brass Mountain) which had been through the Abyssinian Campaign.

ASSINIBOINE INDIAN COUNCIL NEAR FORT WALSH, 1878

OLD FORT EDMONTON, 1879

*SIOUX WIFE OF GEORGE PENBRIDGE N.W.M.P.
AT FORT WALSH, 1878*

Mrs. Penbridge, née Tahnoncoach, was the niece of Sitting Bull.

N.W.M.P. CAMP AT STANDOFF, 1880's. A. G. IRVINE IS PICTURED FOURTH FROM RIGHT

The derivation of the name of the Fort is particularly colourful. It was built in 1872 by Joe Kipp, Charlie Schultz, and Howell Harris; taking with them a supply of liquor from Ft. Benton, their trail was picked up by a lawofficer. Schultz and his companions claimed (rightfully) that the officer was outside his jurisdiction—thus 'standing him off.'

And some ten years later, whiskey traders again appeared in the area, but stood off the Police with a lesser degree of success. The law included Jerry Potts this time and, following a bitter-cold march to Ft. Macleod (during which Jerry and the arresting officers "could only keep from freezing by frequent doses"), a small detachment of Police was formed at Standoff.

N.W.M.P. HORSE CAMP AT GRAYBURN COULÈE, CYPRESS HILLS, 1879

When buffalo herds drifted from their camp, a peaceful existence for the Assiniboine Indians temporarily stopped. But the tribes moved to the Cypress Hills, where they seemed to enjoy a new lease on life.
This was the preface to the Cypress Hills Massacre, an event that was editorialized in the East, and was a major factor behind the founding of the N.W.M.P. And while the first Mountie forts were being built, Sir John A. Macdonald sent instructions to make the necessary arrangements for extradition of the alleged murderers from Montana. It was this fierce desire to bring to trial the perpetrators of the massacre that prompted one of the most exhausting, intensive efforts to find justice. And although 'true' justice was never realized, the efforts of the Police served as a keystone in winning Indian respect and cooperation for a peaceful coexistence.
Commissioned to supervise the extradition of the alleged murderers, Supt. Irvine began his journey under the pretense of 'enjoying western scenery.' From Bismarck Dakota he travelled by Steamboat to Fort Peck, then via the treacherous overland route to Benton, where he secured substantiated evidence. In a state where trials were mockeries, an incredible sympathy was felt for the traders by the locals; the fact that these traders had murdered a peaceful camp of Indians on foreign soil was ignored. Commissioner Macleod made a strong personal appeal for justice, but the outcome of the trial was that the traders could not be extradited because they had had no 'premeditated' design to kill. (And Commissioner Macleod himself was arrested for 'falsely imprisoning' one of the defendants.)
From Montana, Irvine returned to Ft. Macleod where additional members of the gang had been arrested; then, from Ft. Macleod to Winnipeg—the nearest point where a trial could be held—800 miles to the east. From Winnipeg, Irvine retraced his journey back to what he considered "God's Country".
Following this last journey, during which he sustained himself largely on buffalo tongue and prairie chicken, his room, pictured, was, indeed, a welcome sight.

SUPT. ACHESON GOSFORD IRVINE — A PERSONIFICATION OF THE MOUNTIE MOTTO: MAINTIEN LE DROIT

C TROOP AT FORT MACLEOD, 1879

Supt. William Winder is at centre. Yes, these are the men, pill boxes and all, who brought law and order to the wild west.

BULL TRAIN AT FORT WALSH, 1878

KA-AR-O-TON – BEARSHIELD

N.W.M.P. TROOP UNDER CANVAS IN CYPRESS HILLS, 1879

A special comraderie and a love for "God's country" and nature existed amongst the Mounties. Horses and hounds (in rear or frontal views) are represented in many tintypes of the N.W.M.P.
Taken at Ft. Walsh in 1879, this photo depicts, from left to right: (an anonymous dog), Const. Wm. Osler, Const. Chas. Webster and his horse "Tricks", Cpl. G. B. Moffatt.

MOUNTED TROOP IN FRONT OF MAIN GATE, FORT WALSH, 1878
Sgt. Bradley, Insp. Antrobus and Insp. Neale are pictured.

28–MILE SPRINGS, MONTANA, WITH FORT BENTON STAGE IN FRONT, 1878

THE EAST END DETACHMENT, LOCATED AT THE SOUTHEASTERN SLOPE OF THE CYPRESS HILLS, 1879

FORT MACLEOD; CAPTAIN WILLIAM WINDER'S ROOM AT THE FORT

In the formation of a 'new west,' the Irvine administration (commencing 1881) represented a turning point. The west was being made 'liveable'. Typical of this was the fact that, rather than retiring to the east, former Mounties chose to tame their own piece of west. With Supt. Crozier's taking command at Ft. Macleod, Supt. Jarvis retired to Edmonton. In his retirement, William Winder, who preceded Jarvis at Macleod, embarked on a double career of stock ranching and trading.

STAR CHILD, FAMOUS BLOOD WARRIOR AND SCOUT

As a young brave, Star Child was sought by the Mounties for allegedly killing a Mountie. He alluded them for years, until the ubiquitous Jerry Potts caught up with him. After serving a jail term, he was released; thereupon, he became a scout for the Mounties. He always claimed his good luck in life was due to the fact that he never married. But eventually he did tie the knot. He died shortly after the nuptials.

FAR RIGHT: RED CROW, HEAD CHIEF OF THE BLACKFOOT NATION

In 1877, prior to signing the Great Blackfoot Treaty (Number 7), Chief Red Crow had spoken: "Three years ago, when the Mounted Police came to my country, I met and shook hands with Stamix Otokan (Macleod) at the Belly River. Since that time he has made me many promises and has kept them all."

The Chief's loyalty and trust in the "Great White Mother" was evidenced during the early stages of the Riel Rebellion.

I. G. BAKER AND CO., FORT MACLEOD, 1879

As the far west became the 'West,' various tell-tale signs were to signify the increasing growth of the region. An example was a new policy adopted by I. G. Baker and Company. Goods that were formerly imported from Montana were now delivered from eastern Canada (bonded through the United States).

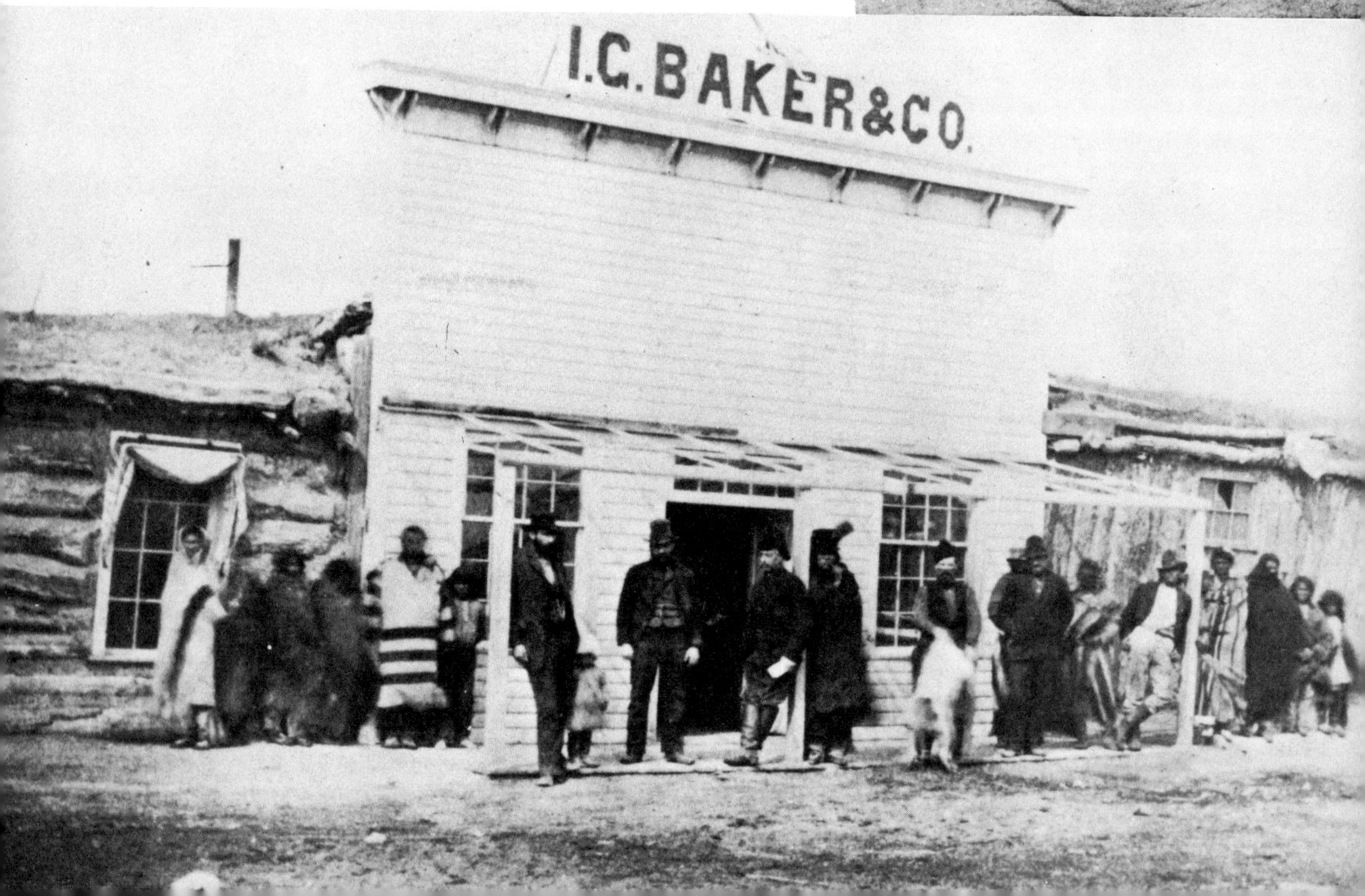

F TROOP N.W.M.P. AT FORT CALGARY, 1876

N.W.M.P. STOCKADE, CALGARY, BOW RIVER, 1881

N.W.M.P. AT GLEICHEN, 1880's

STAGE COACH, WINNIPEG TO ST. BONIFACE, 1879

SUPERINTENDENT PERCY NEALE'S QUARTERS, FORT WALSH, 1880

Chapter 2

As unrest among the Indians and Métis grew in the year 1885, the men of the North West Mounted Police must have felt very isolated and very remote from home. This remoteness from Ottawa played a large part in the rebellion. The government did not seem to comprehend the heartbreak of starvation that was widespread among the Indians with the disappearance of the buffalo, nor the concern of the Métis for their farmland, as settlers and developers began to arrive. The Northwest Rebellion, inevitable in the circumstances, erupted; there was very little that the Mounties could do. Their outposts were not staffed with sufficient men to fight off the large numbers of Crees, Assiniboines and half-breeds who now attacked them. The Blackfoot Confederacy alone remained loyal.

The Dominion government acted finally, and an army arrived from the east to deal with the rebellion. And again the Mountie was to find himself in the most exposed position in this army on lonely patrols and as advance scouts, drawing the fire of the enemy away from the troops. After Riel's capture and the collapse of the rebellion, the N.W.M.P. turned to the work of pacification and the healing of wounds. Government instructors taught the Indians the art of farming and Indian schools were started. Many of the native people settled for this peaceful life on reservations, but there were still young braves who preferred cattle and horse stealing and who preyed upon the increasing number of settlers arriving in a steady stream. The apprehension of these outlaws was carried out by the Mountie with tact and diligence.

Life on the prairie was settling down to steady growth and development.

BLACKFOOT INDIANS AT SHAGANAPPI POINT, CALGARY

THE GREAT INDIAN CHIEF, POUNDMAKER

LEFT: INDIANS DRYING BUFFALO MEAT
Indian life grew more difficult in the Canadian West as the U.S. Cavalry forced American Indians north. One tribe would cut into another's supply of buffalo, upsetting the tender balance of life.

*ABOVE: N.W.M.P. SCOUTS AT QU'APPELLE, 1879
J. Leader, W. Leslie, J. Pringle and Mutch (order not known)*

LEFT: N.W.M.P. SCOUTS AT FORT MACLEOD.

Upper right, Jerry Potts; upper left, Mr. Hunbury; middle row (left to right), Cecil Denny, S/Sgt. Chris Hillard, Sgt. George S. Cotter; front row, Elk Pacing the Wind, Black Eagle, Blood Indians.

So many of the inspectors in the Mounted Police seemed to possess inherent diplomatic capabilities. Inspector Cecil E. Denny was one such prudent mediator whose prompt and personal attention helped to avoid an explosive clash. Informed of the possibility of an attack by the Cree to avenge the murder of a tribesman by a Blackfoot, Denny arrived at the Indian camp. The murderer, Jingle Bells, had fled; the Inspector requested a large council. Cree and Blackfoot were asked to air their grievances and the result was a compromise. The Crees overlooked the murder and the Blackfoot moved their camp and compensated the victim's family. With great ceremony, Chief Crowfoot presented Denny with a magnificent buffalo robe – an expression of respect and earnest gratitude for the Mountie's meeting the Indians on Indian terms. Denny, who had made a point of patiently staying at the camp until a fair solution was reached, best summed up the affair and the significance it carried: "But for a little management, there might have been most serious trouble between these two large camps, and a general Indian war between the Crees and Blackfoot would have followed, which, with our small force, would have been nearly impossible to quell."

RIGHT: COL. JAMES FARQUHARSON MACLEOD

The Blackfoot Treaty of 1877 (Number 7), between the tribes of the Confederacy and the Queen as represented by the Canadian government was negotiated by Hon. David Laird, first lieutenant-governor of the Northwest Territories, and Col. James F. Macleod, second commissioner of the N.W.M.P. It was signed by the principal chiefs of the Blackfoot, Blood, Piegan, Sarcee, and Assiniboine, among them: Crowfoot, Red Crow, Old Sun, Bull's Head, Bear Paw, Heavy Shield, Many Spotted Horses, Rainy Chief, and North Axe.
On October 31, 1880, Col. James Farquharson Macleod (Stamix Otokan) ended his career as a Mountie Officer.

On November 1, 1880, Lieut.-Col. Acheson Gosford Irvine took over the command.

SAMUEL TRIVETT (ABOVE) AND GEORGE McDOUGALL (BELOW)
Both were men of the cloth. The Reverend McDougall's sideline was fur; he was a renowned trapper. The Reverend Trivett was the first Anglican missionary to the Blood Indians.

"THE ROSEBUD"

Among her most important voyages was bringing U.S. General Nelson A. Miles and his corps across the Missouri 'to drive all hostile Indians [in Canada] across the line.'

THE STEAMBOAT "CHEYENNE"

A DETACHMENT OF N.W.M.P. FROM REGINA TO BATTLEFORD

LEFT: CST. "PEACH" DAVIS

Eager to move wandering Indian braves northward from the border camps to established reserves, Commissioner Irvine requested "Peach" (Daniel) Davis to oversee the migration. Davis, well versed in Indian language and character, lead more than 1,000 Indians across uninhabited land. It was a three-week journey, involving internal conflicts and raids. But even the stampeding of the horse herd (with 100 miles yet to go) failed to daunt Peach. He commandeered a horse from a halfbreed in the name of the Queen, and with that horse a courier was able to arrange for a new herd.

For his work, Davis received mention for a duty well-performed, an offer of an Indian squaw by an appreciative Bear's Head (he declined), and, for which he was most grateful of all, a bath and some fresh clothing.

FAR LEFT: PIAPOT, CREE INDIAN CHIEF

In 1882, as C.P.R. construction forged onward, the disappearance of several miles of main line proved a surprise indeed for the surveyors. The disappearance was finally traced to Chief Piapot. It had been hoped that with the railway providing employment, native grievances and problems would diminish. But in the case of Piapot, this proved untrue.

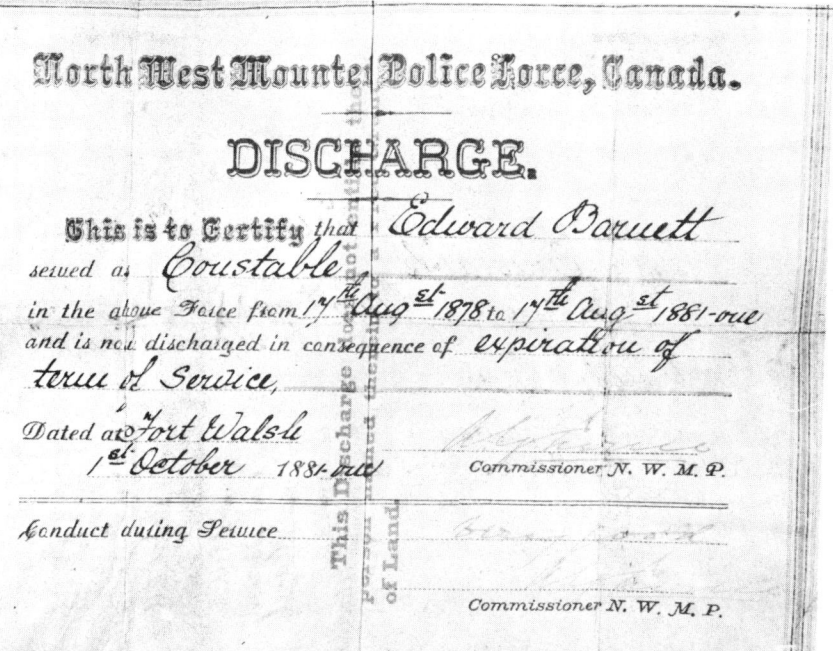

J. H. McILREE, ASSISTANT COMMISSIONER, 1895

LEFT: SUPT. SEVERE GAGNON

As Inspector in North Saskatchewan, Gagnon co-supervised (with Supt. Jarvis) the 3,000 Indians scattered between Edmonton, Victoria, White Fish Lake, Lac la Biche, and Battleford. During the Riel Rebellion, Gagnon commanded Fort Carlton.

In his supervisory capacity during the rebellion, Gagnon was to send two significant communications to Commissioner Irvine. Together, the messages were reflective of the shocking momentum Riel was to build. On January 26, 1885, alerted to the troublesome situation, Gagnon wrote: "[The followers] had a social meeting at which they presented their Chief, Riel, with $60.00 as a token of their good will.... No allusion was made to the present troubles." And on March 26: "Crozier exchanged shots with rebels at Duck Lake. Six men reported shot. Crozier retreating at Carlton."

FORT CALGARY, INCLUDING THE I.G. BAKER AND COMPANY STORE AND THE FIRST HOSPITAL

Fort Calgary was completed in November, 1875. Originally christened Fort Brisebois, it was renamed Calgary (Gaelic for clear, running water) after Macleod's birthplace (Scotland). The fort, which occupied the area between the Bow and Elbow Rivers, was a nucleus activity, around which many settlements grew up, among them those of the Blackfoot and Sarcee.

A GROUP OF N.W.M.P. SERGEANTS

N.W.M.P. CAMP AT FORT WALSH (SASKATCHEWAN), 1878

QUARTER-MASTER SGT. SIDNEY STONE

YOUNG MAN AFRAID OF HIS HORSES

A SIOUX INDIAN HOLDING THE PEACE PIPE

LEFT: KAK-SAY-KWYO-CHIN (SWIFT RUNNER)

A gentle Cree Indian – and a self-confessed cannibal, Swift Runner had been prompted in dreams by the Ween-de-go, or Cannibal Spirit. His crimes were uncovered by Inspector Gagnon and Superintendent Irvine. His menu had included his wife, children and mother-in-law. The execution was described by Californian 49'er Jim Read as "the purtiest hangin' I ever seen and its the twenty-ninth."

METIS SCOUT FOR THE N.W.M.P., 1885
He has a regulation police saddle and his own horse.

RIGHT: BUILDINGS OF FORT SASKATCHEWAN FROM THE BASTION

Chief Factor Richard Hardisty of the Hudson's Bay Company favoured building the fort on the present site of the University of Alberta (i.e., near to the Company). Jarvis vied for erecting the fort at a site that would be nearer to the railway crossing Saskatchewan, a site that offered a better prospect for settlement. The settlement that did grow around Fort Saskatchewan, Saint Albert, was to be saved from poverty and famine through the combined efforts of the Mounties and the local clergy.

Squared pine, handmade shingles, logs, mud, metal stovepipe – and men of fortitude and kindness. These were the elements of Fort Saskatchewan. On more than one occasion did Jarvis praise his Mounties for their "perfect conduct" and "real hard work."

OLD FORT SASKATCHEWAN

ABOVE: FORT PITT, THE DETACHMENT OF WHICH INSPECTOR FRANCIS DICKENS (NUMBER 12) WAS IN CHARGE DURING RIEL REBELLION

Assigned to protect Fort Pitt, Francis Dickens, with his 23-man detachment, was determined to hold his ground against Chief Big Bear. The Indian camp outnumbered the Mounties ten-to-one, and Big Bear, with whom Dickens had been close in former years, sent the Inspector the following plea:

"My dear friend... since I first met you... we have always been good friends.... I do not forget, the last time I visited Pitt he [Commissioner Irvine] gave me a blanket.... I want you all out without any bloodshed.... Try and get away before the afternoon, as the young men are all wild and hard to keep in hand."

This photo was taken before Dickens escaped down the North Saskatchewan River.

FORT PITT, 1884

FORT PITT DETACHMENT, LATE 1884
First row: Cst. John A. MacDonald, Cpt. Charles Phillips, Cst. A. Macdonald, Martin. Second row: Cst. Quigley, Cst. Smith, Cst. Habbs, Cst. D. Gains Third row: Cpt. R. B. Sleigh, Cpt. F. Ledue, Cst. L. O'Keeffe, Cst. J. H. Carrall, Cst. A. McMillan, Insp. F. Dickens. Fourth row: Cst. J. F. Harren, Cst. B. H. Robertson, Cst. Rowley, Cst. Edmund.

INTERIOR OF FORT PITT

Pictured left to right: Fire Sky Thunder, Sky Bird (son of Big Bear), Matoose, Napasis, Big Bear, Angus McKay, Dufrain, L'Goulet, Stanley Simpson, Alex McDonald, Rowley, Corp. Sleigh, Edmund, and Henry Dufrain.

Foreshadowing the North-West Rebellion was a portentious, symbolic display of unrest under the co-directorship of Chiefs Poundmaker and Big Bear. Hoping to bring about a concentration of forces, the chiefs joined to hold the annual Thirst Dance. A threat by a member of the visiting camp (Big Bear's) against a Mounted Policeman triggered a series of grave events during an already tense time.

The police asked that the agitator be brought forward but, painted for the dance, the offender retained his anonymity. Eventually identifying and capturing the man, the Mounted Police were to be further antagonized by the Indian camp. But the police remained steadfast and calm. The following item was reported in the Saskatchewan Herald: "...had one shot been fired, the human mind could not foresee what would have been the result. The courage and coolness (of Crozier) in going amongst the Indians unarmed and alone is deserving of the greatest praise."

Although Big Bear's and Poundmaker's plan of concentration failed on the surface, it was indication enough of what lay ahead. Writing to Ottawa, Crozier warned: "It is poor, yes, false economy to cut down the expenditure so closely in connection with the feeding of the Indians. (The Thirst Dance fight had been instigated by an Indian begging for alms on foreign territory.)"

Ottawa remained seemingly unaware of the imminent danger.

STEELES SCOUTS, N.W.M.P; SEVENTEEN MEN IN UNIFORM, 1885

JOHN HIGINBOTHAM, MOUNTED ON HIS HORSE, CHESTER

Adjoining the fort was the village of Macleod, virtually the capital of the West. In addition to Mr. Higinbotham and Mrs. Morden, prominent residents included numerous retired officers and the Rev. Samuel Trivett, who conducted the first Indian day school.

The Macleod Hotel was run by "Kamoose" Taylor, former preacher and former whiskey trader. His true Christian name was Harry; Kamoose (thief) was a reference to one of his other early achievements — having run off with several squaws.

LEFT: J. D. HIGINBOTHAM'S DRUG STORE IN FORT MACLEOD, 1884

The first drug store in what became the Province of Alberta.

CAPTAIN JOHN FRENCH AND HIS SCOUTS, 1885
The famed "French's Scouts" corps was among the three original groups of Mjr.-General Middleton's force.

MEMBERS OF THE ORIGINAL N.W.M.P. POST, MEDICINE HAT, 1883
Pictured are Sgts. Jim Pearcey and Bob Dechesney

COL. SAM STEELE AND A DETACHMENT OF N.W.M.P. AT FARWELL, B.C., 1885

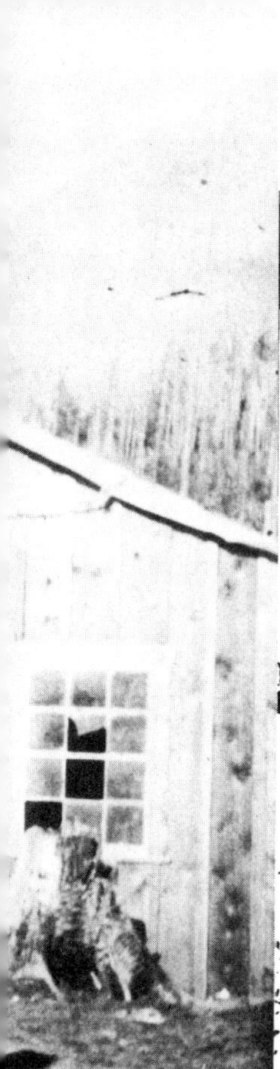

A NOTE WRITTEN TO AN ASSISTANT TRADER OF A HUDSON'S BAY POST

Quinn was shot during the Frog Lake Massacre by an Indian who forced him to write the note.

Please give Miserable Man one Blanket.

T.T.Q.

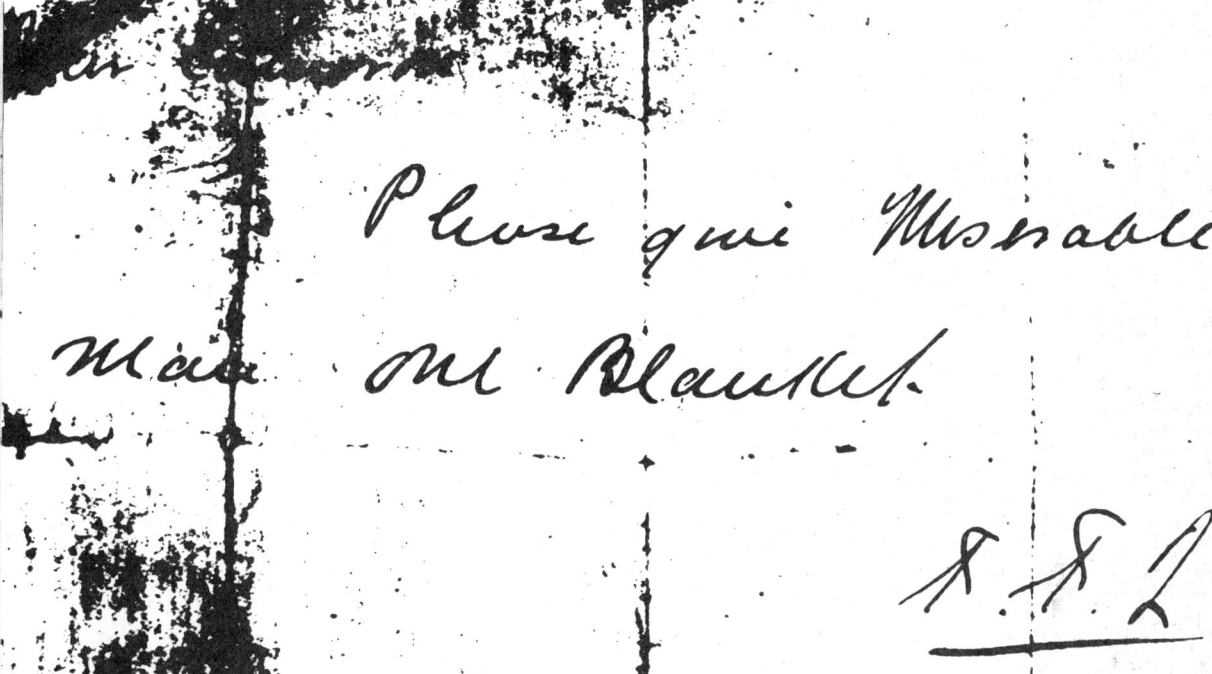

TOM QUINN AND FRANCIS DICKENS (LEFT)

This is believed to be the last photo taken of Quinn before his death.

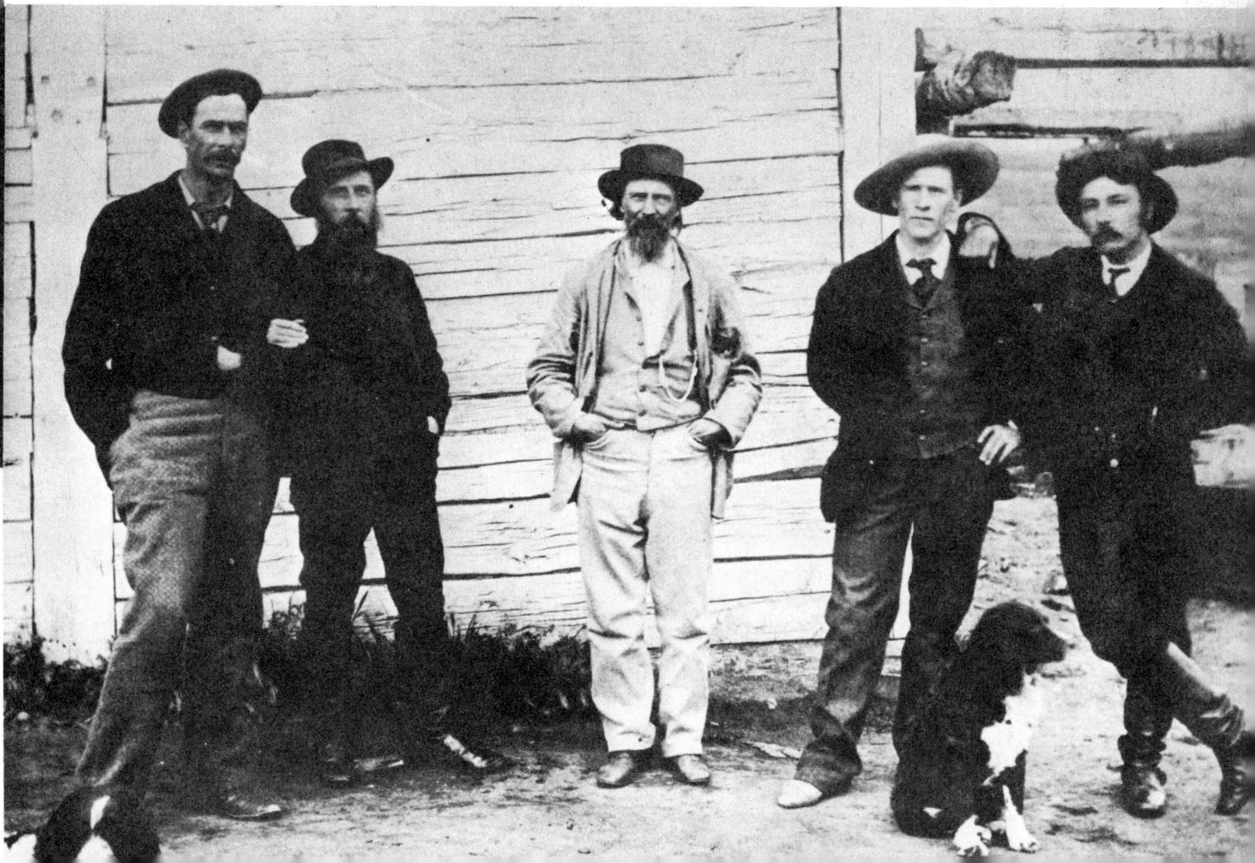

N.W.M.P. POST IN SOUTHERN SASKATCHEWAN

N.W.M.P. DETACHMENT AT DONALD, B.C.

FORT MACLEOD WITH RANCHERS IN THE FOREGROUND; PICTURED ARE E. H. MAUNSELL (LEFT) AND J. McFARLANE (MOUNTED)

BLACKFOOT INDIAN CAMP, 1883

BELOW LEFT: N.W.M.P. AT BANFF, 1880's

IMASEES, SECOND SON OF BIG BEAR
Instigator of the Frog Lake Massacre, he later escaped to Montana.

N.W.M.P. BARRACKS, POLICE POINT, MEDICINE HAT, 1884

Among those depicted are Sgt. Maj. Duchesnay, Jim Weeks, Pete Bertles, Wm. Cousins, S/Sgt. Bethune, McKenzie, Dr. Ballintine, Tho Irland, Jennie Bassett, Mrs. Wm. Cousins (order not known).

LEFT: N.W.M.P. DETACHMENT AT FORT CARLTON

Standing: S M. Dann, Cst. Roberts, Oliver, Littlefield, Doyle, unknown, Westores, Cpt. Pringle, unknown. Second row: Cst. Waite, Manner, Smith, Doc Miller, Supt. Gagnon, unknown, Cst. MacPherson. Third row: Cst. Fleming, Pork, unknown dog, Wilmont, Carter, unknown.

N.W.M.P. DURING THE RIEL REBELLION, 1885

METIS GROUP, 1873

The Riel Rebellion

In 1425 in France, a thirteen year old peasant girl began to hear mysterious voices and to perceive strange visions. She believed that these manifestations came directly from God and that their purpose was to convince her that she had a divine mission and that it was to save France. In 1431 she was burned at the stake by her countrymen. Her name was Joan of Arc.

In the mid-1800's, on the lonely prairie of western Canada a young man with French blood also began to hear mysterious voices and to perceive strange visions. He too believed that he had a divine mission to save his people. He too was executed. His name was Louis Riel.

He was born on October 22, 1844, in a log cabin in what is now St. Vital, Manitoba. His father, Louis Riel, Sr. was himself a radical who in 1849 was to lead the Métis in a 'free trade' revolt against the monopolistic tactics of the Hudson Bay Company. His mother Julie (née Lagimodière), was a deeply religious woman whom he adored. Only one-eighth of his blood was French, the rest was a volatile mixture of Irish and Indian.

He did well at his studies and so was sent to the seminary in Montreal, but it was felt there that he did not possess the necessary humility for the priesthood and he returned to the Red River settlement in 1864.

At this time he was tall, almost six feet, strikingly handsome, with brown waving hair and compelling eyes. His gift of oratory was spellbinding; on occasion he held the attention of his listeners for as long as seven hours.

In 1869, when surveyors from Ontario made their appearance in the colony and began dividing the Métis land into townships, the confused people turned to Louis for leadership in their fight with Ottawa. They set up a Provisional government with Louis as President. The new government occupied Fort Garry until an army arrived from the east and Riel fled to the United States.

The following year the government officially exiled him to the United States for a period of five years.

Modern biographers of Joan of Arc have speculated that she was a victim of schizophrenia and perhaps this is another thing Louis Riel had in common with her. During this period of his life he was twice confined to mental hospitals and on at least one occasion is said to have walked around stark naked proclaiming that he was Jehovah.

Upon his release from hospital he moved into the rectory in Keeseville, New York and there he apparently fell in love with the curé's sister, a Miss Evelina Barnabé. Evelina returned his love and when he left for Montana, sent him many letters proclaiming her affection, until one day when she read in a Montana newspaper of his marriage to an illiterate 18-year old Métis girl.

Louis settled down to a life of domesticity and teaching school in St. Peter's, Montana. It was here that the Métis' delegation found him in June, 1884. They wanted him back they told him, to lead his people again.

Had he declined, the North West rebellion would probably still have taken place. The grievances of the Métis were real and the government in Ottawa was deaf to their pleas.

The Indians were starving, despite the efforts of the North West Mounted Police to feed them. But Louis Riel with his peculiar talents was the man to bring them together, to lead them in battle.

In this, as in everything else that he did, his methods were unusual. On March 19, the feast of St. Joseph, the patron saint of the Métis, he took over the Roman Catholic church at Batoche as his military headquarters, and raised over it a flag bearing a picture of the Blessed Virgin Mary on a white background.

In the opening battle of the rebellion, near Duck Lake, Superintendent L. N. F. Crozier, fifty-six Mounted Police, and forty-one Prince Albert volunteers rode into an ambush. Twelve of Crozier's men died and eleven were wounded. He was forced to retreat. Gabriel Dumont, Riel's Adjutant-General urged him to follow the Mounties and wipe them out, but Riel refused with the words, "There has been too much bloodshed already."

Cree Chiefs Big Bear and Poundmaker were not as ready to listen to words of restraint and there followed savage attacks on white settlements, culminating in the massacre at Frog Lake. Then the Dominion government acted and sent out an army against the rebels. Despite early victories by the Métis and the Indians, the rebellion could not have ended any other way. On May 12, at Batoche, Riel was captured and arrested by Sgt. Smart and Csts. Sullivan, Nichoels, and Kerr of the N.W.M.P. Perhaps even then he could have escaped the hangman had he cooperated with his defence and pleaded insanity, but he said he preferred to die rather than have the Métis cause mocked as the ravings of a lunatic. At the end of the trial he rose and delivered a lucid and moving speech that sealed his fate.

On November 16, 1885, while reciting the Lord's Prayer, Louis Riel was hanged.

Perhaps the parallel between the lives of Joan of Arc and Louis Riel could be carried a step further. In 1920 Joan was canonized a saint of the Roman Catholic Church, her executioner. It seems unlikely that the government of Canada will ever canonize Louis Riel. Still, on October 2, 1968 in Regina, Saskatchewan, the Prime Minister of Canada unveiled a statue to him and on December 30, 1971, another statue of the Métis rebel was unveiled in front of the Manitoba legislature.

LOUIS RIEL

"These people (Indians and Métis) are just as were the children of Israel, a persecuted race deprived of their heritage. But I will redress their wrongs. I will wrest justice for them from the Tyrant. I will be to them a second David."

Riel was above all a symbol – of leadership to the Métis and of insurrection to the government in Ottawa. Perhaps it was his mixed blood (French, Indian, and Irish) that made him a man of contradiction. A deeply devout Catholic who affected flamboyant dress and sometimes bawdy conversation and who toyed with the affections of a priest's sister. A martyr devoted to the Métis cause, but who accepted a bribe of $1,600 from Sir John A. Macdonald to stay out of the country during the elections of 1870.

GABRIEL DUMONT

The outstanding fighter, plainsman, and strategist for the Riel Rebellion, Dumont was commandant in the battles of Duck Lake, Fish Creek, and Batoche. He was known among his people as Ai-caw-pow and was deeply respected not only by his followers. Sir John A. Macdonald was to say of him: "Mr. Gabriel Dumont, I speak of him with respect because he was a brave man although a rebel."

N.W.M.P. CAMP AT QU'APPELLE, 1885

On March 22, 1885, Sir John A. Macdonald officially announced the news of the Riel uprising and the fact that Major-General Dobson Middleton was en route to the West as Commander-in-Chief of all forces. Fort Qu'Appelle was Middleton's headquarters and primary base of operations; once established, he was to divide his force into three columns. The main one trained at Fort Qu'Appelle and pushed northwest to Batoche. A second, under General Otter, proceeded west from Swift Current to Battleford. The third, under Officer Strange, marched from Calgary to Edmonton. Held up by the Métis at Fish Creek, Middleton resumed his march to Batoche where, with the combined assistance of Commissioner Irvine, he ultimately defeated Riel's main force.

TROOPS AT BATTLEFORD, 1885

COL. MIDDLETON'S MEN MARCHING WEST THROUGH TOUCHWOOD HILLS TO HUMBOLDT 1885

CHIEF BIG BEAR AND HIS CAPTORS

THE TRIAL OF LOUIS RIEL

RIEL ADDRESSING THE JURY

THE MEN WHO FOUND RIEL GUILTY

NON-COMMISSIONED OFFICERS, N.W.M.P., 1884
The Calgary detachment that went to Regina to quell the Riel Rebellion.

BLOOD TREE BURIALS, 1886

BLACKFOOT CAMP ON THE PRAIRIE NEAR THE ELBOW OF THE SOUTH SASKATCHEWAN RIVER, 1886

CHIEF OWL, BLACKFOOT INDIAN 1886

NORTH AXE,
HEAD OF THE NORTH
PIEGANS, 1886

N.W.M.P. OF 1886.

*GEORGE LEUASSEUR'S FREIGHTING
OUTFIT, PINCHER CREEK, ALBERTA*

THE REGINA N.W.M.P. POST, 1886
*The officers are, left to right, Begine, Insp. Moffat,
Surgeon Jukes, Supt. Deane, Comm. Herchmer.*

LETHBRIDGE STORE, 1886

N.W.M.P. AT BANFF POST, 1888

N.W.M.P. OFFICERS AT FORT MACLEOD, 1887.
Left to right: Col. G. Sanders, Supt. Casey, Capt. John "Paper Collar Johnny" McDonald, Col. Samuel B. Steele, Howard, Wroughten, Morris.

The Officers' Spring Fashion Show in Regina was always a big hit. Here a group of officers model the latest in uniforms as well as the spiffiest civilian fashions of that wonderful year, 1888. Left to right: standing, Insp. S. Routledge, Nathan, Moffatt, Norman, Supt, Cothan, Insp. MacPherson; seated, Supt, Jarvis, Insp. Constantine and son.

BAND OF "E" DIVISION, N.W.M.P.

Left to right: front row, Joseph Gilhespie, Cst. F. K. Sewell, Trumpeter W. R. (Shaky) Hunt, Cst. H. Alnutt, bugler; middle row, Cst. W. J. Ritchie, Cst. W. Boyle, S.Sgt. F. A. Bagley (bandmaster), Trumpeter A. B. Baird, Cst. G. W. Carrier; back row, Cpl. S. L. Saunders, Cst. Tom Agnew, Cst. J. (Shorty) Davis.

*SUPT. MACDONELL A. R. ENLISTED, JULY, 1876;
COMMISSIONED, JANUARY 9, 1878*

DRILL INSTRUCTOR PAT MAHONEY, 1886

EARLY PRAIRIE SETTLERS
A wagon team near Qu'Appelle en route to Alberta area from Russell.

RIGHT: RUNNING DEER, A CROW INDIAN ALSO CALLED HOOP ON THE FOREHEAD

FAR RIGHT: WHITE BULL, A CROW INDIAN

BELOW: MAPLE CREEK, SASKATCHEWAN, LATE 1880's

A GROUP OF NINE RANCHERS

SERGEANTS N.W.M.P., REGINA, 1890

Left to right: back row, Sgt. Pennefather, Staff Sgt. Lasswite, Sgt. Garnham, S/Sgt. Tulloch, Sgt. Pigott, Sgt. Matheson, S/Sgt. Samuel Horner; middle row, S/Sgts. Martin, Hopkins, Des Barres, Sgt. Major Belcher, S/Sgt. Woodward, Sgt. Huntley, S/Sgt. Flindt; front row, S/Sgt. Graydon, S/Sgt. Mason.

ARTILLERY DETACHMENT "D" AND "H" DIVISIONS N.W.M.P. UNDER THE CAREFUL EYE OF INSP. Z. T. WOOD; DECEMBER 17, 1890, FORT MACLEOD, N.W.T.

SPRING DRILL OF N.W.M.P. AT REGINA, 1890

THE FASHIONS OF THE DAY CALLED FOR THE BEST-DRESSED WOMEN TO BE GARBED IN THE STYLE DEPICTED BY MRS. HARRISON YOUNG OF EDMONTON

COL. S. B. STEELE, COMMANDING OFFICER OF LORD STRATHCONA'S HORSE, IS SHOWN HERE AS SUPERINTENDENT OF N.W.M.P., IN CHARGE OF MACLEOD DISTRICT

In the 1890's, revisions were being made regarding Mountie dress and equipment. Supt. E. W. Jarvis opted for the small calibre Smith and Wesson revolvers to replace the Enfield variety. And Supt. Steele was of the strong opinion that the left side was too awkward for a mounted man to carry his revolver. He felt that a holster-alteration was required, and he objected to the practice of carrying the carbine across the horn of the saddle (it prevented perfect dressing). In his efforts to modernize the uniform, Steele gained some fame for his recommendation that the red serge be abolished: "No man however tidy can keep one clean and tidy for three months," he remarked.

N.W.M.P. OFFICERS' FOUR-HORSE TEAM, MAPLE CREEK, 1890's. GEORGE B. MOFFAT AND SON ARE STANDING AT RIGHT

The Maple Creek post occupied a strategic position: midpoint between Regina and the newly occupied Fort Steele, B.C. post.

N.W.M.P. BAND, REGINA

MAIN STREET OF MACLEOD

Main street in the new "boom town," Macleod. W. J. Ryan has identified the landmarks: Looking at the photo, you are at the north end of the street, facing southwesterly. The slough is about two hundred yards south of the town. The Old Man's River is on the west of town. Turning to the right, on the north of town, it is some hundred yards to the N.W.M.P. barracks, going easterly towards Lethbridge.

Among those shops on the left is the I. G. Baker Co. Warehouse and James Scott's Livery stable. The I. G. Baker Co. store, Harry Taylor's Billiard Hall, Taylor's restaurant and F. Kanouse's 'log dispensary' (opened in 1882) are among those buildings on the right.

C.P.R. STATION AT MEDICINE HAT. THE PHOTO SHOWS TWO DIFFERENT UNIFORMS OF THE N.W.M.P.

Chapter 3

There are many reasons why the frontiers of civilization attract the adventurous. Not the least of these is the hope of quick profit. In 1895 the first wave of what was to become a flood of miners and prospectors arrived in the Yukon in search of gold. The Mounties, under the command of Inspector C. Constantine, were not far behind. They first established a post at Fort Cudahy on the Yukon River, then the most northerly outpost in the British Empire. On September 24, 1896 their strength was twenty officers and men and they represented the government in all its departments. Constantine, as mining recorder, routinely signed the applications of George Washington Carmack, Taghish Skookum Jim, and Taghish Charlie for claims embracing a new discovery of gold "on a creek known as Bonanza Creek and flowing into the Klondike River." The greatest Gold Rush of all time was on.

As gold-fever spread, the need for more police grew, until in 1898 there were twelve officers and 254 men in the Yukon, which in that year was constituted a separate territory by Act of Parliament, with a population of 20,000. With the move to the far north, a new type of recruit entered the force, the team dog. Reports written at this time speak of the difficulty in obtaining sufficient numbers of good dog teams to cover the vast areas involved in the many duties carried out by the Mountie. In one year 64,000 miles were covered while delivering mail to the scattered mining camps.

But even a task of that magnitude must have seemed easy compared to the maintenance of law and order in Dawson and Skagway. Skagway was described by one of the officers who served there as "a hell on earth" where "murder and robbery were daily occurances" and where "men were seen frequently exchanging shots in the street".

After the end of the South African War, settlers came to the western prairies in large numbers. Some 300,000 people became homesteaders during a short period. And in the Yukon a census showed a population of 16,000 whites. At this time the Yukon detachment was increased to 300 men and new posts were set up in the Sub-Arctic.

In 1904 King Edward VII officially recognized the work done by the Mounties by granting them the use of the prefix "Royal" in their name and they became the "Royal Northwest Mounted Police".

In 1905 the provinces of Saskatchewan and Alberta were created to join with Manitoba to form the prairie provinces. This move into the 20th Century did not mean that the Mounties' work was over. An insight into the magnitude of their duties at this time is found in their records: "An Inspector with a corporal and three constables, leaving Fort Saskatchewan on a morning in early June, 1908, headed northward to Fort Resolution on Great Slave Lake, crossed the vast, unfriendly wilderness to Hudson Bay, employed Eskimo dogs to Churchill, and eventually reached Lake Winnipeg in the following spring, a distance travelled of 3,347 miles."

N.W.M.P. SCOUTS AT FORT MACLEOD, MOUNTED, DECEMBER 20, 1890

Left to right; Sir Cecil Denny, Black Eagle and Elk Facing the Wind (Bloods), S/Sgt. Chris Hilliard, Sgt. George S. Cotter, Scout Hunbury.

A GROUP OF STONY INDIANS AT MORELY WITH THEIR LEADER, MARK KNOHAY

SUPT. CONSTANTINE (FOURTH FROM LEFT, BACK ROW) AND N.W.M.P. AT SELKIRK

SGT. W. B. WILDE AND MEN OF THE PINCHER CREEK DETACHMENT, 1895

A few men in a small post could cover hundreds of miles, keeping law and order at a low overhead. Pictured here are, left to right, Cst. Gould, Scout Holloway, Cst. Willis, Sgt. Wilde, Csts. Ambrose, Burder, and Hatfield.

PORCUPINE DETACHMENT, N.W.M.P.

In the Porcupine Hills are, left to right, Csts. Connors and MacDonnell, Sgt. Watson, and Cst. Lewis.

SGT. HALLIDAY, N.W.M.P., 1895

PROCLAMATION.

ABERDEEN.
(L.S.)

CANADA.

VICTORIA, by the Grace of God, of the United Kingdom of Great Britain and Ireland, *Queen*, Defender of the Faith, &c., &c.

To all to whom these presents shall come, or whom the same may in anywise concern,— GREETING:

A PROCLAMATION.

E. L. NEWCOMBE,
Deputy of the Minister of Justice, Canada.

WHEREAS, on the twenty-ninth day of October, one thousand eight hundred and ninety-five, **COLIN CAMPBELL COLEBROOK**, a Sergeant of the North-West Mounted Police, was murdered about eight miles east of Kinistino, or about forty miles south-east of Prince Albert, in the North-West Territories, by an Indian known as "Jean-Baptiste," or "Almighty Voice," who escaped from the police guard-room at Duck Lake;

And Whereas, it is highly important for the peace and safety of Our subjects that such a crime should not remain unpunished, but that the offenders should be apprehended and brought to justice;

Now Know Ye that a reward of **FIVE HUNDRED DOLLARS** will be paid to any person or persons who will give such information as will lead to the apprehension and conviction of the said party.

In Testimony Whereof, We have caused these Our Letters to be made Patent and the Great Seal of Canada to be hereunto affixed.

Witness, Our Right Trusty and Right Well-beloved Cousin and Councillor the Right Honourable Sir JOHN CAMPBELL HAMILTON-GORDON, Earl of Aberdeen; Viscount Formartine, Baron Haddo, Methlic, Tarves and Kellie, in the Peerage of Scotland; Viscount Gordon of Aberdeen, County of Aberdeen, in the Peerage of the United Kingdom; Baronet of Nova Scotia, Knight Grand Cross of Our Most Distinguished Order of Saint Michael and Saint George, &c., Governor General of Canada.

At Our Government House, in Our City of Ottawa, this Twentieth day of April, in the year of Our Lord one thousand eight hundred and ninety-six, and in the Fifty-ninth year of Our Reign.

By command,

CHARLES TUPPER,
Secretary of State.

DESCRIPTION OF THE AFORESAID INDIAN "JEAN-BAPTISTE" OR "ALMIGHTY VOICE":

About twenty-two years old, five feet ten inches in height, weight eleven stone, slightly built and erect, neat small feet and hands; complexion inclined to be fair, wavey dark hair to shoulders, large dark eyes, broad forehead, sharp features and parrot nose with flat tip, scar on left cheek running from mouth towards ear, feminine appearance.

ASSISTANT SURGEON CHARLES S. HAUTAIN

Assistant Surgeon Hautain saw medicine enter the twentieth century. Of the N.W.M.P. who helped bring the science to the 1900's, one man, Dr. J. Kittson, stands out. As the autumn of 1879 approached, Dr. Kittson, Fort Walsh surgeon, noticed typhoid ("mountain fever") symptoms in the village as well as in the fort. The mortality rate was particularly high among halfbreed and Indian children. What was exceptional was that the fever should strike at an altitude (3400 feet above sea level) where infectious diseases were virtually unknown. A thorough examination of the water supply showed that Battle Creek ran through putrified swamps. Rains yielded overflows of the mainstream. Kittson's isolation of the source was discussed in his report: "A noxious cesspool was found in a blind alley... where the sergeant's cook was in the habit of throwing slops... overcrowding of the huts was no doubt an important factor.... Experience has taught us that each of a body of men occupying one room should be allowed at least 600 cubic feet."

In 1879, Dr. Kittson's suggestions were put into effect; a well was dug, serving as the exclusive source of drinking and cooking water.

There were hospitals at Regina, Maple Creek, Medicine Hat, Lethbridge, Calgary, and Prince Albert. Hautain was one of five assistant surgeons (to Jukes). There were eight qualified veterinary surgeons in the force.

WILLIAM AND THOMAS CAREY AND FAMILIES, CANMORE

William Carey is wearing the fashionable bowler. Thomas sports the tam.

MACLEOD DISTRICT HEADQUARTERS
The officers are, left to right, Sanders, Oliver, E. B. Steele, Casey, Norman, Davidson, Wroughton. The helmet, although it had its own uses, was soon to be honourably discharged for softer head wear.

"C" TROOP, BATTLEFORD, N.W.T., 1895

SUN DANCE TENT NEAR BATTLEFORD

The sun dance was a religious offering practised by all Plains Indians. An annual ritual, it would follow the ceremony that marked the test of manhood. It was attended regularly by members of the Mounted Police, who checked that the frenzied rites stayed within "civilized bounds." It is hardly fair—or even possible—for an objective observer to describe or to understand the dance. The ritual fused all the senses: drums and chanting; the aromatic burning of the purifying sweet grass; the feasting; the spectacularly embellished dress. All this preceded the youth's ordeal: wooden skewers with weights piercing the muscles—all endured with incredible stoicism.

OLD WOMEN'S SOCIETY LODGE, BLOOD RESERVE

WRITING-ON-STONE DETACHMENT, N.W.M.P., 1897

SGT. WILDE'S FUNERAL PROCESSION, IN FORT
MACLEOD, PASSING THROUGH 24th STREET, 1896

ST. MARY'S DETACHMENT, 1897; CST. COTTER AND CST. BRUCE

CST. BAGSHAW, N.W.M.P., AT KOOTENA DETACHMENT IN SOUTHWESTERN ALBERTA, 1897

N.W.M.P. POST IN BANFF. NOW PART OF HERITAGE PARK

CALF-BRANDING AT PINCHER CREEK ROUND-UP, 1886

THE FIRST TRAIN INTO EDMONTON SOUTH, JULY 25, 1891

LAYING TRACK FOR SIDING NEAR FORT MACLEOD, 1897

A GROUP OF MEN LINED UP OUTSIDE
THEIR HEADQUARTERS, DAWSON, Y.T.

PEOPLE WERE THE REASON F
THE MOUNTIES' MOVE
NORTHWARD AND WESTWARD

The boom town of Dawson in July, 1
shows why law and order were the
coming things.

CHRISTMAS DINNER AT THE DAWSON POST
The maxem gun had an honoured place in the dining room. Here it was kept warm—and kept close to the parade ground.

THE CHANGING OF THE GUARD
As early as 1899, tourists would flock to the Dawson post to watch the event.

A POSED PHOTOGRAPH CALLED "GODDESSES OF LIBERTY ENLIGHTING (ENLIGHTENING) DAWSON, Y.T."

WOMEN OF DAWSON, Y.T.

SNAKE-HIPS LULU, A KLONDIKE DANCE-HALL GIRL, 1898

N.W.M.P. AT PINCHER CREEK, 1899

BLOOD INDIANS POW-WOW AT N.W.M.P. BARRACKS, FORT MACLEOD, JUNE 28, 1898

TWO STONY INDIANS IN WINTER DRESS; PETER (LAST NAME UNKNOWN) AND PHILIP HOUSE (RIGHT), 1900

BLACKFOOT INDIANS GATHERED AT THE AGENCY FOR THE VISIT OF LORD MENTO, 1900

A N.W.M.P. ESCORT FOR THE TREATY COMMISSIONERS, 1899

A GROUP OF INDIANS GATHERED ON THE OCCASION OF THE ROYAL VISIT, 1901

CROWD GATHERED AT SHAGANAPPI POINT, CALGARY, FOR THE VISIT BY THE DUKE AND DUCHESS OF YORK IN 1901

N.W.M.P. MOUNTED ESCORT, CALGARY, 1901

TWIN LAKES R.N.W.M.P. DETACHMENT
AND CUSTOMS STATION, SOUTH OF
CARDSTON, 1904-10

MIKE WALKER, THE FAMOUS TURN-OF-THE-CENTURY COWBOY

CORPORAL BOWLER ON HIS HORSE "BURY BILLY," 1904

The photo was taken on an advance party of a N.W.M.P. expedition between the mouth of Little Slave River and Lesser Slave Lake.

JIM RYAN ON A BUCKING HORSE; THE BROWN RANCH, QUEENSTOWN, EARLY, 1900's

HENRY GEORGE, A SURGEON TO
THE N.W.M.P. AT CALGARY

George was in attendance at the death of Crowfoot, 1890.

MANY SHOTS,
A BLACKFOOT INDIA
1900

A BLOOD INDIAN WITH AN AMERICAN FLAG AS A WAR TROPHY, 1900

BATTLEFORD BARRACKS, "C" DIVISION, R.N.W.M.P., 1905

Middle row, on bench, left to right: Sgt. Major. A. H. Richardson, V.C., Insp. T. McGinnis, Commanding Officer, Supt. A. C. Macdonnell, Asst. Surgeon de Martingy, Staff Sgt. F. W. Light.

Chapter 4

A difficult time of decision came for many individual men of the R.N.W.M.P. with the outbreak of war in 1914. The work they were performing at home became in many respects even more important, but the pull to enlist in the regular army was strong. Many chose to enlist, so many in fact that by 1918 the strength of the force was reduced to 303—almost the same as that of the pioneer force of 1874. Much of their activity had to be curtailed in Alberta, Saskatchewan and northern Manitoba in order to concentrate on the urgencies of patrolling the International Boundary and surveillance of aliens in the country.

At the end of the war the government decided to make the R.N.W.M.P. a permanent force with a strength of 1,200 and assign to it jurisdiction over the whole of Canada west of the Lakehead. In 1920 that jurisdiction was extended to include the entire country and the name of the force was changed to the Royal Canadian Mounted Police. The force absorbed the Dominion Police and their headquarters was moved to Ottawa.

At the time of their 50th Anniversary in 1923 their strength was 1,148 men. They celebrated their anniversary by again breaking new ground in the far north. A post was established at Craig Harbour in Ellesmere Land—then the nearest British post to the North Pole.

THE GRAVES OF THE MEMBERS OF THE LOST PATROL

CORPORAL W. J. D. DEMPSTER, DAWSON CITY, YUKON TERRITORY, 1911

The photo was taken shortly after Dempster and his relief crew had located the remains of the lost patrol.

MOSES BEARSPAW, HEAD CHIEF OF THE STONY INDIANS, 1908

G TROOP AT FORT SASKATCHEWAN, 1906; UNMOUNTED, MOUNTED

MOUNTIES LEADING THE PARADE FOR THE GLEICHEN STAMPEDE, 1915

FREIGHTING ON THE OLD CARIBOO ROAD, BRITISH COLUMBIA, 1911

JOHNNY ONE SPOT, SARCEE SCOUT FOR THE MOUNTED POLICE, 1914

BLACKFOOT INDIANS PARADING AT EXHIBITION GROUNDS, CALGARY STAMPEDE, 1919

HOLT.   FIELD.   WALSH
SONIER   HOPE.

THE STETSON HAT BECAME A PART OF THE MOUNTIE UNIFORM ON JANUARY 1, 1901

MOUNTIES AT THE FIRST CALGARY STAMPEDE, 1912

Postscript

The second half of the Mounties' century bears little resemblance to the first. Much of their work will always be the same. This is a huge country and much of it is still wilderness; much of the Mounties' work even today is carried out in the wilderness.

But if Commissioner George A. French and Commissioner James Macleod were alive today they might be mildly surprised to learn that the journey from the Lakehead to Fort Garry that took them two months under unbelievable conditions of hardship can now be done in one hour and five minutes in the sumptuous luxury of a jetliner. They might also be surprised to learn that the R.C.M.P. do not have to depend on commercial air travel, but have their own Air Division of sixteen planes and a Marine Division of sixteen patrol boats on the Pacific coast, fifteen on the Great Lakes and eight on the Atlantic coast with an additional complement of 302 small craft.

Superintendent L. N. F. Crozier and Inspector Francis Dickens would be reassured to know that today's Mountie still apprehends smugglers and murderers, but they might be puzzled to hear that the smuggler's main stock in trade today is narcotics and that murderers are tracked down by complicated evidence processed in modern laboratories. But after the initial shock wore off, these early heroes of the force would probably ask one question and the answer they would hear would reassure them. The Royal Canadian Mounted Police, no matter how much their methods have changed, are still one of the most efficient, effective and respected police forces in the world.

Chronology

Formation of the North-West Mounted Police	1873
Lieutenant-Colonel French appointed Commissioner	1873
Mounties reach Fort Whoop-Up	1874
The Force's first arrest	1874
Establishment of Fort Walsh	1875
The Cypress Hills Massacre	1875
Lieutenant-Colonel Macleod appointed Commissioner	1876
Headquarters established at Fort Walsh	1876
Sitting Bull and refugee Sioux enter Canada	1876
Signing of the Great Blackfoot Treaty (No. 7)	1877
Lieutenant-Colonel Irvine appointed Commissioner	1880
Birth of the C.P.R.	1881
Headquarters moved to Regina (Pile of Bones Creek)	1882
The North-West Rebellion	1885

    The Battle of Duck Lake
    Destruction of Fort Carlton
    Frog Lake Massacre
    Evacuation of Fort Pitt
    Engagement at Fish Creek
    The Fall of Batoche

Trial and Execution of Louis Riel	1885
Lawrence W. Herchmer appointed Commissioner	1886
The Yukon Gold Rush	1897-1898
Modernization of uniform	1901
Granting of prefix "Royal"	1904
The Lost Patrol (McPherson-Dawson)	1911
Force relieved of provincial police duties in West	1917
Force becomes "Royal Canadian Mounted Police"	1919
Force absorbs the Dominion Police	1920

Credits

Photographs by kind permission of the following:

Manitoba Archives

Pp. 54 and 55, 156.

The Public Archives of Canada

Pp. 137 (C-20301), 162 and 163 (C-1876), 224, top (C-18642), 224, bottom (C-14478).

Provincial Museum and Archives of Alberta, The Ernest Brown Collection

Pp. 66 and 67 (B-592), 82 (B-5202), 83 (A-283), 136 and 137 (B-2481), 150 (A-284), 158 (B-215), 220 (M-1086), 242 and 243, top, 242 and 243, bottom.

Glenbow-Alberta Institute

Pp. 1 (NA-65-2), 2 and 3 (NA-917-6), 10 and 11 (NA-237-10), 18 (NA-98-11), 20 and 21 (NA-716-9), 28 and 29 (NA-65-4), 31 (NA-544-82), 34 (NA-34-1), 36 and 37 (NA-68-1), 42 (NA-500-18), 42 (NA-550-11), 42 (NA-555-2), 53 (NA-583-1), 56 and 57 (NA-98-16), 60 (NA-659-57), 61, bottom (NA-1071-1), 62 and 63 (NA-98-27), 70 (NA-98-14), 71 (NA-644-1), 72 and 73 (NA-98-15), 74 (NA-7902), 75 (NA-136-1), 81, bottom (NA-1196-7), 84 and 85 (NA-52-1), 86 (NA-98-13), 87 (NA-136-2), 88 (NA-936-34), 89, bottom (NA-935-1), 90 (NA-659-26), 91 (NA-936-12), 92 (NA-307-1), 94 and 95 (NA-98-18), 96 (NA-790-5), 97 (NA-790-1), 98, top (NA-98-12), 99 (NA-136-4), 100, top (NA-936-15), 101, bottom (NA-98-26), 102, top (NA-451-1), 103, bottom (NA-98-24), 104 and 105 (NA-659-16), 106, bottom (NA-944-4), 107 (NA-936-7), 110 and 111 (NA-539-4), 114 (NA-556-1), 115 (NA-936-2), 116, top (NA-659-71), 116, bottom (NA-589-1), 117 (NA-18-5), 118 (NA-532-1), 119 (NA-944-2), 119, top (NA-936-23), 123, bottom (NA-284-6), 126, top (NA-1038-1), 128, top (NA-1183-6), 128, top (NA-102-15), 128, bottom (NA-504-1), 130 (NA-635-2), 131, bottom (NA-936-3), 133 (NA-935-4), 136 and 137 (NA-1193-9), 140 and 141 (NA-936-22), 142 (NA-670-9), 143, top (NA-670-52), 145 (NA-363-5), 146 (NA-294-1), 148 (NA-1071-2), 148 and 149, top (NA-944-9), 149 (NA-782-3), 150 (NA-659-27), 151 (NA-925-1), 152 and 153, top (NA-315-1), 159 (NA-1063-1), 166 (NA-1081-3), 167, top (NA-1081-2), 170, top (NA-896-2), 171, top (NA-716-5), 174, bottom (NA-936-32), 175, top (NA-1087-3), 175, bottom (NA-922-3), 176 (NA-842-2), 180 and 181 (NA-673-12), 182 (NA-1071-3), 183 (NA-307-2), 184 and 185 (NA-923-2), 187, bottom (NA-1196-3), 188 and 189 (NA-919-10), 191, bottom (NA-659-23), 192 (NA-1030-11), 193 (NA-118-55), 194 (NA-919-2), 195 (NA-1171-1), 196 and 197 (NA-967-41), 198, bottom (NA-1160-1), 200 and 201, top (NA-936-9), 200 and 201, bottom (NA-1171-12), 202 and 203 (NA-919-15), 204 and 205 (NA-936-8), 205 (NA-936-11), 206 (NA-125-9), 209 (NA-967-45), 213 (NA-936-31), 214 (NA-943-19), 215 (NA-943-20), 216 and 217 (NA-670-8), 218, top (NA-943-22), 218, bottom (NA-1156-1), 219, top (NA-936-39), 219, bottom (NA-943-26), 221 (NA-943-45), 222, bottom (NA-912-5), 223, top (NA-174-2), 226, top (NA-659-88), 226, bottom (NA-1075-11), 227, top (NA-1122-10), 227, bottom (NA-118-13), 228 and 229 (NA-949-3), 230 and 231, top (NA-1075-17), 231 (NA-919-14), 232, top (NA-936-14), 232, bottom (NA-740-5), 233 (NA-494-2), 234, top (NA-740-2), 234 (NA-583-2), 234 (NA-103-56), 235 (NA-769-11), 238, bottom (NA-513-41), 239 (NA-695-40), 242 (NA-915-38), 242 and 243 (NA-313-1), 243 (NA-26-6), 243 (NA-923-3), 246 (NA-440-3).

Greenhill/Miller Services
p.30

Every effort has been made to acknowledge sources. Any omissions or errors brought to our attention will be amended in subsequent editions.

The author is especially grateful to George S. Howard of Islington, Ontario, for his advice and counsel. Mr. Howard is an ex-sergeant of the R.C.M.P., and for many years was in charge of all official publications.